talking mathematics

Co-principal investigators

Rebecca B. Corwin
TERC and Lesley College

Susan Jo Russell
TERC

Writers

Judith Storeygard
Sabra L. Price
Anne Goodrow
Gene Novak
Paula Hooper

Support staff

Sara Burke
Frederic Evans
Elizabeth Ferry
Catherine Call

talking ≈ mathematics

Supporting Children's Voices

Rebecca B. Corwin
with Judith Storeygard & Sabra L. Price

HEINEMANN *Portsmouth, NH*

Heinemann
361 Hanover Street
Portsmouth, NH 03801-3912
Offices and agents throughout the world

Credits for borrowed material appear on page 167.

Library of Congress Cataloging-in-Publication Data

Corwin, Rebecca B.
    Talking mathematics : supporting children's voices / Rebecca B.
Corwin with Judith Storeygard and Sabra L. Price.
        p. cm.
    Includes bibliographical references (p.   –   ).
    ISBN 0-435-08377-5 (acid-free paper)
    1. Mathematics—Study and teaching (Elementary)   I. Storeygard,
Judith. II. Price, Sabra. III. Title.
QA135.5.C636   1995
372.7'044—dc20   95-34652
                                                            CIP

The Talking Mathematics project was undertaken with the support of National
Science Foundation Grant No. TPE 9153793. Any opinions, findings, conclusions,
or recommendations expressed in this publication are those of the authors and do
not necessarily represent the views of the National Science Foundation. These
materials shall be subject to a royalty-free, irrevocable, worldwide, nonexclusive
license in the United States Government to reproduce, perform, translate, and
otherwise use and to authorize others to use such materials for Government purposes.

Acquisitions Editor: Toby Gordon
Copy Editor: Alan Huisman
Production Editor: Renée M. Nicholls
Cover Designer: Jenny Jensen Greenleaf
Cover Photo by John Guare, Film Cell Photography

Printed in the United States of America on acid-free paper
Docutech RRD 2009

Contents

Preface

Mathematics is probably both the most loved and the most hated school subject. People often tell stories about when and why they decided they couldn't do mathematics. Although there is some shame in these stories, there is also anger. Why didn't "they" do a better job teaching me? Why did "they" give up on me? Why was I labeled "incapable"?

Mathematics educators need to take these questions very seriously. For over a century North American schools have been teaching computational arithmetic in the elementary grades. In high school, algebra is a transitional course to "more interesting" mathematics. But by then many students have decided or been told that mathematics is not for them.

One of the most daunting roadblocks for students is the constant emphasis on following procedures rather than on inventing, expressing, or fiddling around. This myopic concentration on arithmetic and on rote memorization and speed is detrimental to many. For some students, geometry reveals the beauty and power of mathematics for the first time. For others, algebra is a liberating experience that teaches a way of representing and working with variables. But for most, these subjects come too late or not at all. The predominant notion of mathematics is drill, tests, and humiliation.

One way to change this is to adopt a more exploratory, investigative perspective in elementary school so that students learn to think about mathematical situations, to pursue their own ideas, and to develop effective strategies with regard to number, space, and data. Rather than present a body of predetermined knowledge to be mastered, we want to develop a curious, problem-posing habit of mind.

Many teachers are therefore rethinking their approaches. As a way to support this kind of professional reflection and change, we have created a collection of resources for teachers, staff developers, inservice providers, and university instructors. The collection comprises this book for classroom teachers, seven twenty-minute videotapes about mathematical communication in elementary school classrooms, and instructional resources for facilitators to use in seminars.

The materials in this book—some theory about why mathematical talk is important, practical ways to encourage and support that talk, a set of pertinent readings, a few problems to try with students, and a list of resources—support teachers (and teacher education students) who are interested in developing a culture of inquiry and communication in their mathematics classes.

Producing these materials required the support and efforts of many people. We have, of course, fallen in love with many of the children whose mathematical talk is captured here. Without their excitement and openness and their willingness to participate, there would be much less to offer you.

The teachers who took part in the seminars through which these materials were developed came from many school systems and grade levels. We list them in our acknowledgment section. Nothing can express our gratitude for their energy and openness. Working with these thirty-seven people reminded us every day of the high level of intelligence, sensitivity, and commitment that are the backbone of the schools.

As we came to know teachers and students as mathematicians, we were constantly reminded of the truth of one teacher's inspired comment: "Mathematics belongs to the people who are doing it." These students and teachers were indeed members of mathematical communities who invented and understood mathematics for themselves.

Acknowledgments

Many thanks to the teachers who participated in the Talking Mathematics project:

Group One:

Maria Campanario-Araica
Rafael Hernandez School
Boston, MA

Rose Christiansen
Lincoln School
Brookline, MA

Karen Economopoulos
Fayerweather Street School
Cambridge, MA

Barbara Fox
Maurice Tobin School
Cambridge, MA

Linda Kaeding
Special Needs
Chelsea/Framingham, MA

Betsy Lake
Devotion School
Brookline, MA

Elizabeth Lieber
James Otis School
Boston, MA

Teresa Lloyd
Henry Grew School
Boston, MA

Hilory Paster
Lincoln School
Brookline, MA

Jo-Ann Pepicelli
Curtis Guild School
Boston, MA

Lourdes Santiago
Rafael Hernandez School
Boston, MA

Cynthia Schwartz
James W. Hennigan School
Boston, MA

Group Two:

Rosaly Aiello
Alcott School
Concord, MA

Audrey Barzey
Early Learning Center West
Boston, MA

Edith Baxter
Hartwell School
Lincoln, MA

Joanne Berger
Agassiz School
Cambridge, MA

Carol Birdsall
Alcott School
Concord, MA

Sandra Budson
Horace Mann School
Newtonville, MA

Rebekah Eston
Hartwell School
Lincoln, MA

Lynn Faugot
Cambridge Friends School
Cambridge, MA

Steven Glickel
John F. Kennedy School
Boston, MA

Marguita Jackson-Minot
James W. Hennigan School
Boston, MA

Elie Jeremie
Kenny School
Dorchester, MA

Sally Kelly
Henry Grew School
Boston, MA

Robert Lemaire
Thoreau School
Concord, MA

Ruth Levey
Hartwell School
Lincoln, MA

Michael Marino
Lynch Elementary School
Winchester, MA

Liz Miller
Maurice Tobin School
Boston, MA

Amy Morse
Atrium School
Watertown, MA

Sarah Novogrodsky
Longfellow School
Cambridge, MA

Michelle O'Bryant
James W. Hennigan School
Boston, MA

Priscilla Rhodes
Hartwell School
Lincoln, MA

Janice Rook
Maurice Tobin School
Boston, MA

Caral Walker
Horace Mann School
Newton, MA

Marina Seevak
Agassiz School
Cambridge, MA

Lucy Wittenberg
Fayerweather Street School
Cambridge, MA

Paula Tranchita
Lincoln School
Winchester, MA

There are others to thank: the National Science Foundation, which funded the work with teachers that made everyone's professional growth possible; the schools and systems that released their teachers from the classroom so they could participate; our families, who tolerated our being late getting home and spending hours watching rough drafts of videotapes once we got there.

Finally, this project would have been impossible without the constant support of our friend and editor, Toby Gordon, who went out of her way to support the development of the complete resource collection. We are indebted to her for her enthusiasm, intelligence, and attention to detail.

Introduction

"What's the biggest number in the world?"
"Are negative numbers like shadow numbers?"
"Who invented fractions, anyhow?"
"Are the numbers the same backwards as forwards?"
Early in their lives children ask questions about numbers that are exploratory, playful, and investigative. They try things, convince themselves, and move on to their next question and then to their next investigation. But those questions stop somewhere along the line and seem to vanish, perhaps because of what children learn about mathematics in school.

None of us wants to discourage students from pursuing their own investigations in mathematics. But we allow precious little time for students to communicate and express themselves mathematically in some of the same ways that are so supported in their literacy classes. It is understandable—we did not learn to see mathematics as a communicative social act, so it is difficult to support our students when their mathematical creativity and engagement produce something to communicate about. There is still in most of us a gulf between what we think of as language and what we think of as mathematics.

We assume a child will "correct" her early mistakes in talking. We assume a child will learn to walk even though he falls repeatedly in the process. When a child thinks she's ready to ride a bicycle, we try to help her, even though we may believe she's still too young.

But we worry differently about mathematics. We have learned (wrongly) that there is one progression to mastering mathematics. In order to add, we must know the number facts. In order to divide, we must already be able to add, subtract, and multiply. Missing-addend problems like $4 + \square = 7$ must be solved using subtraction.

Our educations did not give most of us a sense of number as a *human invention*. Anonymous ancient Greeks usually get credit for inventing pieces of mathematics, but *every* child who understands that there is always one more number or realizes that the third in the row is always after the second and before the fourth or sees that ⅗ is the same as dividing five into three parts has invented mathematics. It's not surprising that our students think of mathematics as cut-and-dried and definite; we are presented with mathematics as "a dead-body thing."

The trouble is, mathematics isn't cut-and-dried. People who do mathematics are people who talk, who fiddle with models and numbers and symbols, who take things apart and try to reassemble them. They turn things around, they name them, they make assertions, they argue. It's a very lively dialogue.

In *Curriculum and Evaluation Standards for School Mathematics* (National Council of Teachers of Mathematics 1989) a cross section of mathematics educators assert their vision of how things need to change. Many believe that the teaching community needs to revive a sense of communication and invention in elementary school mathematics. A more inventive, constructive approach to mathematics can produce students who are powerful, who have a sense of number and shape, and who believe that they can do problems they have not previously encountered.

It is essential that students learn to record their mathematical ideas and communicate them to others. For that to happen, they must encounter situations that lead to mathematical investigation and also require communication. The thrust of current changes in mathematics curriculums involves *finding good investigations* to pursue. Simultaneously, it is important that everyone *learns more mathematics* in order to support children's mathematical growth. Finally, we need to *support students' talk* as they incubate, test, and begin to assert their ideas.

These goals may seem sensible, but they are far from easy to achieve. Even when students have good ideas and are willing to talk about them, how do we decide what directions to pursue with the group? When a problem leads unexpectedly to a debate, how can we support students' mathematical arguments, and separate the mathematical pieces from the just-plain-argument pieces? When a student poses a question that seems obstructionist, we need to be able to reflect on what that child may mean. All of this takes time, thought, and energy.

INTRODUCTION

.... xv

As the staff of the Talking Mathematics project worked with teachers who were exploring how to create classroom cultures that supported mathematical inquiry and mathematical talk, it became apparent that there is more than one way to achieve these goals. Teachers worked hard to make sense of what was happening in their classrooms when they tried different ideas and different problems with their students.

At the beginning, the group bonded strongly as they did mathematics for themselves. They enjoyed working together and found that doing their own mathematics was an essential part of creating a mathematical community. Teachers also studied their own teaching via videotapes and transcripts. They brought questions and concerns to the group so that everyone could reflect on pedagogical issues.

It was also important for the group to develop shared images of the classroom. As they acquired a history and a set of shared referents, their conversations deepened. Teachers tried things with their own classes and raised questions about their teaching and their students' mathematical thinking. This sense of community was a crucial element in the teachers' professional experience. It became a touchstone for many of them.

But how could we use our experiences to support teachers who were not members of the seminar? Was it possible to develop a set of resources that might help classroom teachers grapple with some of the same questions? Were there ways to capture images of teaching for others to discuss? What elements of the Talking Mathematics experience might be helpful to others?

There were certain resources that seminar members used as benchmarks:

- *Doing mathematics together*, pursuing mathematical investigations focused on specific problems.
- *Reflecting on their own mathematical thinking* as a way to find their mathematical identities.
- *Reflecting on teaching techniques* as they talked about their own mathematical learning, shared classroom videotapes with one another, and discussed professional articles and their own essays and journal entries.
- *Reflecting on children's mathematical thought* as they observed classroom interactions and listened to students talk about mathematics.

We decided to assemble these resources in a format that would help other teachers as they in turn supported their students' mathematical communication by centering their classroom on children's mathematical discourse. *Talking Mathematics in the Classroom* is the result. (We also developed complementary resources for staff developers and university instructors to use with groups in inservice seminars and university classes.)

Section 1 focuses on the theory behind mathematical talk and provides some background about the thinking that lies behind efforts at changing the way we teach mathematics. It emphasizes the parallels between acquiring language in general and acquiring mathematical language. Section 2 highlights ways you can support your students' discourse, become a researcher in your classroom, and explore your students' learning. Section 3 consists of selected readings about doing and teaching mathematics that the classroom teachers in the Talking Mathematics project found especially meaningful. Section 4 is a short series of problems to try as you begin exploring mathematics. We recommend you do them yourself or with colleagues before you do them with your students. Finally, there is a list of other resources and references—effective materials, useful books and videotapes—and where to find them.

A supplementary videotape, *Talking Mathematics: Supporting Classroom Discourse*, can be used in conjunction with this book. It shows classrooms that emphasize children's mathematical talk in action. We hope you can see it. You can also discuss the tape with a group of colleagues or show it to parent or community groups to give them an idea of what it is you're attempting in your classroom.

The best way to support children's discourse is to listen to their thinking and to encourage their questions and exploration. We want all our students to enjoy the journey through mathematics as well as the end products. It will take a lot of cooperative group work, manipulative materials, open-ended questions, and reflection, but it's worth the effort.

Supporting students' mathematical discourse will not, of course, transform every child into a flexible mathematician. Nevertheless, looking closely at children's work and listening attentively to their ideas can change your sense of mathematics and how you teach it. And many students become more involved in mathematics and more excited with their own mathematical questions when they are encouraged to do mathematics, talk about it, and enjoy it.

If possible, do and reflect on mathematics in conjunction with colleagues. It can be a powerful help. As one teacher suggests, "Taking a math course is a great thing—not a course that tells you how to teach it but helps you while you *do* it. That had a huge impact on me."

Working with others to do mathematics and to reflect on it can produce a truly different understanding of the image of mathematics. As David Hawkins (1980) puts it in his essay "Nature, Man and Mathematics"

> What is at stake is not the nature of the end-product usually *called* mathematics, but of that whole domain in which mathematical ideas and procedures germinate, sprout and take root, *and* in the end produce the visible upper branching, leafing and flowering which we here all so value, and which wither when uprooted. (113)

Above all, we want everyone to know that mathematics is not dead. It lives, grows, and develops both in individuals and in cultures. One Talking Mathematics teacher captures it well:

> Somebody wrote about the idea you have as a kid or as an adult that math was like a dead-body thing, that it had already been figured out. That was what it was like for me, when I was in school. Once somebody got the answer, it was dead. And if I didn't understand it, we just went on to the next dead body. And now, I really don't feel like that any more. . . . It's still out there floating somewhere for me. It's not over, dead, and I didn't get it, just one more thing that goes in *that* pile. That kind of thinking just doesn't really exist for me any more, and that's a tremendous, tremendous pleasure.

All of us connected with the project hope that your experiences as you try new ways of teaching and learning mathematics give you that same kind of pleasure.

....

Some Talk About Talk

In social studies and language arts, it seems natural to encourage students to express their thoughts and opinions, to make presentations, and to debate and defend their ideas. In contrast, in mathematics students are often passive; they are expected to learn conventional algorithms, theories, and proofs. Not until recently have students been actively encouraged to construct their own mathematical ideas and engage in discourse.

When most of us learned mathematics, we were expected to master an expert vocabulary quickly, which was confusing at times. We may remember trying to understand what "the commutative property" meant; perhaps we had to scramble to remember what exponents were. Younger children are also confused by terms that are too abstract. Words like "plus" or "equals" can leave children uncertain about what is really meant. To communicate about mathematics we need to use language that matches our ideas and our actions. The words need to be easily accessible.

Curriculum and Evaluation Standards for School Mathematics (NCTM 1989) and *Professional Standards for Teaching Mathematics* (NCTM 1991) describe a vision for improving mathematics teaching and learning. These recommendations for change were developed over a period of years by representatives of both teaching and mathematics communities. In general, they focus on making elementary school mathematics less arithmetically based and procedure-oriented, broader and more oriented to solving complicated problems.

A major recommendation is that we teach mathematics as a form of communication. At first that may seem puzzling. Traditionally, mathematics is seen as a ritual for solving computational problems that have little connection to daily life. Students learn to do computations, to

1

solve some story problems, to read graphs, and to recognize and measure shapes. Usually no one talks or writes about mathematics—in fact, talking in mathematics class is often called "cheating."

But mathematics as a field of study includes a great deal of discussion, debate, and dialogue. Mathematics is created constantly and must be posited, tested, defended, extended, and accepted or rejected by the mathematics community. The silent, diligent computational work we did in elementary school bears little resemblance to the real endeavor of mathematicians. The complications and complexity of mathematical ideas make mathematics a very human activity, involving communication in all forms.

If our students learn to do mathematics silently, they may find that they don't have words readily available to describe mathematical ideas. If asked, What does it mean to do division? a student may give an example: It's like 36 guzinta 895. Students give us the words they know—sometimes rote memorizations. The more students memorize *our* words, the less likely they are to have their own. How did you do it? often leads to a shrug, How did you know? to, I don't know—I just knew it.

It's too easy to forget that children need many, many experiences to develop language fully, even in mathematics classrooms. Children may learn arithmetic procedures by repetition alone; if so, their only tool for recalling how to find solutions is their memory. Mathematics, rather than resting on a rich base of exploration, discovery, conversation, and common sense, may rest exclusively on the relatively weak platform of memory. If it does, students' concepts are not robust enough to be used flexibly.

Participating in mathematical conversations is central to developing strong mathematical ideas. Talking allows students to compare their methods and discuss their ideas and theories with their classmates. Classmates' questions or counterassertions often force a student to examine her own mathematical concepts and ideas. When students begin to comment on each other's methods and ask each other questions, confusion is clarified. Expressing their assumptions in the context of a conversation helps students articulate and refine their ideas.

What Is a Mathematical Conversation and Why Is It Important?

It is hard to imagine a mathematical conversation, especially one that takes place in an elementary school classroom. So here are a few examples.

FIG. 1   The square pyramid.

Four first graders are working with a square pyramid made of plastic. Jason is writing down everyone's comments as the group recorder. As they talk, they pass the model of the pyramid back and forth (see Figure 1).

Ms. B: Look at the shape and write down anything you can tell each other.

Cathy: Let me feel the point on the top.

Jason: Okay! Now—a square.

Jon: Jason, what are you spelling?

Jason: Okay. That's a rectangle.

Cathy: It's a triangle!

Jason: A rectangle!

Kaisha: No, it's a square! I mean, no, um, pointy—

Cathy: Triangles have one, two, three sides. One, two, three, four. A triangle has four sides.

Jon: It has a pointy top.

Jason: It has four sides. I know how to spell that.

Kaisha: And it's got a point on top.

Cathy: And it gots a smooth bottom.

Kaisha: It has stripes up the sides.

Cathy: And it gots a pointy top at the bottom . . . it gots little stripes.

Jason: Wait a second! It has one little stripe over . . .

Cathy: And there's big triangles and little triangles.

Jason [laughing]: Where do you *see* that?

For these students, the key features of this square pyramid include a pointy top, four sides, stripes (we might call these edges), the bottom (or base), and the triangular shapes of the sides. Because they have talked with one another about this solid shape, their collective understanding is richer than any individual's would be. This playful, relatively calm talk is an important step in mathematical discourse, in which students compile their ideas and build a shared description of a mathematical concept, relationship, or object.

In contrast, in the next example fourth graders are being asked about the features of a square. Think about the kind of thought this discourse supports.

Ms. F: What is this called?
Kiku: A square.
Ms. F: What is this called?
Jamie: Rectangle.
Ms. F: This one part of the square is called what?
Raina: Divider?
Ms. F: Well, what is it? What's the name we say?
Maura: Poles?
Jimmy: One half?
Ms. F: One half of the whole, but what is this called?
Minou: Divisor.
Sandy: Divisor.
Ms. F: No, wait a minute. What is a square?
Ann: Four corners.
Ms. F: Four corners and what? [*Silence*] These are the corners. What are these called?
Jamie: The sides.
Ms. F: Sides. All right, so these two corners are connected by?
Students: Sides?
Ms. F: A side. Okay.

These questions ask students to recall and recite facts Ms. F has previously presented to them. Talk is closely directed and there is little room for students' own ideas. The children are fishing for what the teacher wants them to say. They do not seem to be making sense of what they are being asked, but rather they fill in the blanks in "right answer" questions. Being right, in this lesson, means knowing what the teacher wants.

The belief that students must make sense of what they do has touched most of the elementary school curriculum. Many preservice education students learn ways of supporting students' thinking and problem solving as they work toward their certification as teachers. They are encouraged to develop meaningful contexts for student learning rather than teach skills in isolation. Phrases such as "hands-on learning" or "minds-on learning" are frequently used to describe such an inquiry-based approach.

A good example of this shift can be seen in the changes in language arts instruction over the past decade. Writing instruction used to be (and still is, in many classrooms) a read-my-mind exercise. Students' writing was done for the teacher and followed the teacher's rules. It was seldom used to communicate ideas to a broader audience and was centered on topics generated by the teacher alone. Corrections were made by the teacher and usually focused on the form of the work, not the content. Similarly, reading was often taught by stressing decoding skills and using phonics. Understanding was not always the focus of instruction; it was assumed to come as children matured. Many children left elementary school believing that reading existed in workbooks; they did not have any experience in shaping and enjoying language, either in writing or in reading.

Now, however, a new approach to literacy, sometimes called a whole language approach, has become an important paradigm. It is based on the assumption that children need to make sense of what they do. Such an emphasis on making meaning requires a great deal of communication *in a real context*. Isolated drills and memorized rules are no longer the common coinage; instead children are encouraged to learn to read by reading and to learn to write by writing. Understanding and communicating an idea to another person are at the center of the literacy curriculum. Meaning takes precedence over correct form, especially at the beginning. Expression is central; children invent spelling rather than stop writing to find a word. The goal is to connect thinking and writing. Children are encouraged to revise their writing over time. Correct spelling and grammar are still important but are seen in a context of making meaning.

Many mathematics classrooms today are like the skills-based writing classrooms of thirty years ago. It is not surprising that studies of mathematical achievement in our country show that our students can compute but cannot apply knowledge to real-life problems—they learn early on that school mathematics and informal mathematics are quite separate (Ginsburg 1986). The focus of much classroom mathematics is on getting the right answer, and teachers monitor students' work until students learn how to do the computations correctly.

As educators move away from thinking that the whole of mathematics is arithmetic computation, mathematics teachers are beginning to change their pedagogy. Gradually a sense-making approach is coming to be valued in elementary school mathematics. Certainly the National Council of Teachers of Mathematics' vision of mathematics as communication and meaning making has increased the emphasis on talk, writing, and *using* mathematics to solve problems in real contexts. More teachers see the benefits of taking such an approach, but there is much more work to be done before we have a clear understanding of how to teach mathematics so differently.

Viewing students as active participants in their own learning underlies the goals for staff development in elementary mathematics. We want to support the creation of contexts conducive to problem solving, thinking, communication, argument, and sense making, and one of the key elements in this reform is a reconsideration of the role of language in mathematics instruction.

> The development of a student's power to use mathematics involves learning the signs, symbols and terms of mathematics. This is best accomplished in problem situations in which students have an opportunity to read, write and discuss ideas in which the use of the language of mathematics becomes natural. As students communicate their ideas they learn to clarify, consolidate, and refine their mathematical thinking. (NCTM 1989, 6)

There are many benefits to emphasizing mathematical discourse featuring communication, reasoning, and making connections. When teachers incorporate open discourse into their mathematics teaching, they often find natural connections to other subject areas. The following teacher, a bilingual specialist, describes her experience in one classroom she supervises:

> One of the main things is taking a step back, as far as being the talker, to let the children express themselves, to ask the questions, to take the fear of right and wrong out of them. Those things you can apply to everything. . . . I was in a classroom and I was reading

a book about seasons. . . . The kids were really confused; the first graders didn't know what spring was, and [their teacher] was having a fit. . . . I said, "No, wait, let them figure it out." And they did!

What Role Does Talk Play in Mathematics Classrooms?

The medium of mathematical expression is human language. Mathematics is a specialized language developed over centuries to communicate about particular aspects of the world. Mathematical knowledge develops through interactions and conversations between individuals and within their community. It is a social activity.

One way of participating in a mathematics community is through talk. Students use language to present their ideas to each other, build theories together, share solution strategies, and generate definitions. Children's conversation is playful, urgent, and mathematical—they exchange observations, clarify their own and others' ideas, agree, disagree, and challenge one another. By talking—to themselves and to others— students form, speak, test, and revise ideas.

The give-and-take of regular discourse is mathematical when it focuses on communicating mathematical ideas. It may not take a unique form and may seem almost casual at times; mathematical talk ranges along a huge continuum from informal to formal. As it becomes more formal, mathematical talk assumes specialized characteristics (asking for examples, citing proofs) that are rarely present in children's mathematical talk.

The role of talk in schoolchildren's mathematical development has been underrated. Classroom talk plays many roles that are more complex and varied than previously thought. Talk is both individual (we talk to ourselves) and social (we share ideas with others); it is a major avenue for developing and negotiating shared meanings. It must also be broadly defined. Language may be written, drawn, gestured, or spoken.

For example, a group of fifth graders have been working on a fraction problem: If we have five brownies and eight people, how can we share the brownies evenly? How much will each person get? The teacher is trying to follow Tyrone's thinking.

Tyrone: Since there were five brownies and eight people, there were five brownies [*draws them*] and eight people. And if we split them into halves, that's two, one, two, three, four, five, six, seven, eight—now everybody has a half a brownie. Right? And we're going to divide this into eighths. So that's four . . . all right, now it's in eighths. So everybody gets one and a half and an eighth.

Ms. C: One and a half?

Tyrone: And an eighth. One half and an eighth.

Ms. C: Write down what everybody gets.

Tyrone: One and a half [*he writes* ½] . . .

Ms. C: One half . . .

Tyrone: . . . and an eighth. So everybody gets a half and an eighth. And the final is three eighths, we reduced it to.

Ms. C: How did you get three eighths?

Tyrone: You want to do it, Kaisha?

Kaisha: What we'll do is we'll add one eighth and one half, and, since two goes into eight, we can just make both the denominators eight, so we won't have to change this one. When we did two times four to get eight, we do one times four is four, and then we did eight times one is eight and one times one is one. One and four is five, so I guess it was five eighths. So I guess our assumption was wrong.

This interaction shows students revising their ideas and rethinking their assumptions. As Tyrone hears himself describe his strategy, he catches flaws in his notation system and revises his words. Kaisha throws out her original error as she talks through the procedure again; she is completely unflustered by correcting her work "on the fly."

Teachers can model this process by sharing their own thinking as they work through problems: students see that solutions are not instantly foreknown, that everyone may have to grope for an answer, and perhaps most important, that trial, error, and false starts are part of doing mathematics. In the example below, Ms. R, a seventh-grade teacher, becomes interested in finding all the possible combinations of five digits:

Ms. R: So let's see . . . I wonder what would happen with five?

Angela: We'd get more.

Ms. R: This is going to be wicked. [*To the class*] Do you want to find out what would happen with five digits or are you fed up? Tell me the pattern.

A Student: 1 4 3 2 5.
Another student: 1 5 3 4 2.
Ms. R: So the next one is 1 3 5 2 4.
[Students call out more possibilities, and Ms. R records them.]
Ms. R: Oh, why did I open my big mouth? Well, I tell you what is going to happen. This is going to take an immense amount of time.
Soreya: Let's finish tomorrow.
Ms. R: If we could find out how many choices per number. . . With four digits there were six choices, with three digits there were—do you know what I'm thinking—I think I'm the only one thinking. With four digits there were six choices. We found that out because we did it; I wonder if there's a way of figuring out how many choices per number.
Robby: Five times five—twenty-five of them.
Ms. R: No, because that one was—four digits gave six choices—this one is obviously more than that. We have sixteen so far.

Ms. R has been captured by the problem. She is thinking aloud, trying to make sense of it for herself. She and eight of the students begin to bat one another's ideas around and think aloud about the mathematics. This is refreshing for everyone; students rarely see their teachers as coparticipants, posing their own questions and struggling for solutions.

A teacher's use of mathematical terms is also a powerful model for children. Not only are they guided to the words that fit the ideas they are expressing, but they hear and gradually internalize words that embody important mathematical features they may not have noticed themselves. In this way, students build the mathematical concept first, then match it to the appropriate conventional term when they are individually ready. Encouraging talking aloud is one way of putting mathematical terms out where your students can take hold of them.

In a combination first- and second-grade classroom Sam announces that he made a mistake and is trying to figure out what he did. Mr J. asks, "Can we figure out how Sam is thinking?"

Danielle: You can make it easier by saying eighty-three and you need to minus a ten and a seven. So take away a three and that is eighty and then a four is seventy-six. Then ten is sixty-six.
Sam: So, here is my question—why do you take away a three and a four and not a seven?

Danielle: To make it easier.
Mr. J: How much did you take away, Sam?
Sam: Twenty.
Mr. J: Look at the problem.
Sam: I should have taken away seventeen.
Mr. J: Do you see why they are saying you took away too much?
Sam: Yes, but I don't know how.

As he tries to understand his own thinking, Sam is also trying to understand what other students did. He is interested in their methods and is learning to compare his work with others so that he can discover approaches that are more effective. The teacher helps him listen to other students and reflect on his own thought process.

Students internalize classroom mathematics conversations as models for both thinking and problem solving. The process of talking about ideas may be as important as the ideas themselves. Students may adopt another's strategies; they may work through problems in a particular order; they may learn the phrases that will help them keep track of their work. For example, while some fifth graders are working on one of the geometry worksheets from the "Pyramids" problem, their teacher tries to develop their geometric vocabulary:

Ms. T [holding up a square pyramid]: How can you talk about the relationships between the point and edge?
Jaime: Two edges run into a corner.
Daniel: I think the edge is between two corners.
Ms. T: You think an edge is between two corners.
Minou: I think an edge is where faces meet at the end of the face.
Ms. T: Let's see if it works for every edge.
Deborah: Is the bottom considered a face?
Ellie: I don't think that bottom would be considered a face because in our definition of a pyramid, we said that the faces are triangular.

These students have learned to challenge one another's ideas, to scrutinize definitions to see whether they are adequate. They speak about their thought processes and remember what their assumptions were and how their ideas may need to change. As they share more ideas, they internalize the vocabulary needed to talk about the shapes they are by now very familiar with. Edges, faces, corners (all important terms) are full of meaning for each student, since they have been so much a part of their collective experience.

When students "talk math" they communicate their thinking, providing an opportunity for the teacher to glimpse what they are learning. Their written work may convey relatively little about their complex processes of thinking and problem solving; talk is an important medium for understanding students' learning. When students talk about their work, their thoughts often become more evident, enabling teachers to better assess their understanding. Here is how one teacher expresses it:

> Conversations are one more evaluative tool I can use to see where they are, because I spend a whole lot more time asking kids why. When they do something I ask why. Why did you do this? Rather than [my] just correcting things. Lots of times what they write down is something they copied off someone else's book. And if I challenge them about it I can find out if they really don't understand it. So it's part of my taking time to understand the kid's thinking.

These illustrations are just some of the roles talk may play in mathematics classrooms. More will emerge as students are given more sustained opportunities to talk and when discourse is more valued by everyone. Supporting talk gives everyone the opportunity to reflect on mathematics from a variety of perspectives.

By sharing their approaches to doing problems and their strategies for finding solutions, children become more confident about recording and displaying information. They learn to value their approaches, sometimes for the first time, and to enjoy writing, modeling, talking through their ideas and comparing their ideas with others'. Once students realize that mathematics is more than simply finding answers, when they learn to value many ways of doing problems, the possibility of many solutions becomes interesting and reasonable. This cuts down on competition to find the best way of solving a problem or being the first to get an answer.

How Can Teachers Bring a Culture of Inquiry into the Mathematics Classroom?

Our mathematics teachers always seemed to express only clear, complete, unhesitant ideas. The proofs, theorems, and explanations they gave us were absolute and often elegant. This kind of mathematical discourse seemed unattainable given what we knew to be our own clumsy speech.

Too often students today have similar experiences. Because students' speech is relatively unpolished, perfect models of mathematical discourse seem a world away. Our students are unaware that even professional mathematicians do not speak in final form the first time they discuss an idea. Hearing adults openly revise their mathematical thinking can help combat this misconception; so can hearing their classmates' ideas and learning to value their own.

But students who have not participated in mathematical discourse may feel unprepared to contribute to the kind of conversation we have been describing. Here are some teachers' observations:

> Seeing that they have never had it before and never had the opportunity to be small risk takers, I haven't come as quickly as I would have liked to a point where they are talking math and thinking. They're not risk takers, that's the thing, it's not that they don't have that ability to talk, they're afraid to take that risk.

> It's hard with the little ones . . . I see talking math as making your discovery and then defending it, defending your convictions and you see different people bringing in different ways of thinking. I don't see that quite yet in my class. They aren't at the point of questioning each other about their points, and I think this is something that will take time.

Indeed, taking time is one of the most important aspects of creating a mathematical community. If speed is valued over understanding, and if questions are seen as an annoyance, a culture of inquiry cannot develop. Teachers and students alike must be clear that the heart of their mathematics work lies in

- Finding and investigating relationships.
- Recording their ideas.
- Sharing their ideas with their colleagues and classmates.
- Reflecting on the mathematical ideas they are investigating.
- Reflecting on their own mathematical processes.

Real conversations happen when people listen to, respect, and value each other's comments. Mathematical conversations help create a community; in fact, it is often *through* talk (remember, that means gestures, signs, and writing as well as discourse) that students are brought into that community. Because mathematics is socially constructed, new ideas become important community referents. Saying ideas out loud (or producing them in some other way) makes them public property; once stated, classmates can question assertions, react to them, and build from them. Students need to use their own vocabularies at first; insisting too early on the formal language of mathematics may give everyone the notion that mathematics is mostly a set of words, rules, and definitions rather than an exciting domain to be investigated and made sense of.

To increase students' ownership of their mathematics, many teachers acknowledge children's contributions by naming rules or patterns after them:

Kerry: When we do it with rods, if ten is on the bottom it's a plus. If it's on the top it's a minus. Seven plus three equals ten. [*Applause*]

Ms. V: There's Kerry's rule! You found a rule, too. You used the same three numbers. Cathy and William found the switch rule [*that you can switch the addends in addition: 5 = 3 + 2 and 5 = 2 + 3*]. Using that rule, can anyone tell me another plus sentence? Sam?

Sam: Three plus seven equals ten.

Jose: I'm going to do Kerry's rule!

Students who are acknowledged for inventing rules and whose classmates use their rules or strategies to solve problems have a stake in the mathematical process. They know that it is possible to create mathematics and to own some piece of it. This goes a long way toward modeling mathematics as a human invention.

Teachers can also help students learn *how* to talk mathematics by modeling patterns of discourse:

> [Helping students to talk] might involve me modeling some of the kinds of arguing, some of the kinds of questioning that they will eventually own themselves—if they hear it enough they will do it.

What Kind of Talk Should Teachers Support?

Traditionally, mathematics teachers focus on arithmetic computations and the language in their classrooms is relatively unreflective. Typically the teacher explains procedures and then reviews by asking questions. Students recite the correct answers. In the kind of mathematics classroom we have been describing, language is much broader. It includes conjectures, refutations, explanations, and reflections.

In order to develop a mathematical community, teachers need to support talk that:

- Communicates mathematical ideas. Although talk can serve many other purposes in classrooms, in mathematics it is mainly used to convey ideas.
- Is focused and grounded in mathematical experiences. This means that classroom talk centers on mathematics that is being proposed or developed.
- Moves away from the specific context. Students' ideas are expressed in ways that begin to move toward the general.

There are many ways for teachers to encourage talk:

- Help children put their embedded understanding into words or explain their investigations in clear language:

    Ms. G: What statement can you make about a trapezoid and a hexagon?
    Ben: One half.
    Ms. G: That's not a statement.
    Ben: Red is one half of yellow.
    Ms. G: Let's use the words.
    Ben: A trapezoid is half of a hexagon.

    Ms. C: Who would like to talk first about something that they did?
    Sandi: We split our whole bunch into little groups and then we added it all together.
    Ms. C: Explain to me what you mean, little groups?
    Sandi: You swing a little bit over to the side and then you push

away the others. Then we counted. We added them all up.
We added up all the colors.

Ms. C: Explain that again. You counted them and separated them
into colors.

Sandi: We separated them into colors and then we counted them
all up and then we got forty-one as our total.

- Participate in mathematics conversation without dominating,
  letting students feel the conversation is their own and that they
  don't have to direct all ideas to the teacher for approval:

Before, when I was sitting with a small group I'd say, What are you
doing? I'd just come around and ask, What's going on around here?
and they'd explain to me what's going on. Now sometimes I just
sit there and the only time I get involved is to say occasionally,
Give so-and-so a turn. I gave them a lot of leading questions before,
while now I let them struggle and just follow their thinking [as
they talk].

- Model ways students can incorporate active listening into their
  conversations and small-group work.
- Pay attention to the mathematical content rather than the
  form. This helps keep everyone focused on meaning rather than
  grammar. At times it may be useful to introduce new
  mathematical terms or formal language, but this is not
  productive early in talk about new ideas.
- Seize opportunities and act spontaneously, following up on the
  unexpected comment or question that may initiate a
  discussion.
- Have students discuss a problem or idea in small groups before
  the whole group convenes:

If you're alone with nobody to talk to or discuss it with, you forget
it. You drop it. Working with the group, even if I didn't do it that
way, it was an opening to starting my own thinking. I do think
that has helped. I've noticed it with the kids, too. If they're working
alone they'll just automatically, if they don't understand, go to each
other even if they do it differently. It's just a way of opening up
their thought processes.

- Refer students' questions to the class and wait before reacting to students' ideas. This encourages student-student interaction and shifts the focus of conversation away from the teacher as authority.
- Be careful about wait time. Even a three-second pause after a question encourages more and deeper participation (Rowe 1987).

References

Ginsburg, H. 1986. *Children's Arithmetic: How They Learn It and How You Teach It.* 2d ed. Austin, TX: PRO-ED.

National Council of Teachers of Mathematics. 1989. *Curriculum and Evaluation Standards for School Mathematics.* Reston, VA: National Council of Teachers of Mathematics.

———. 1991. *Professional Standards for Teaching Mathematics.* Reston, VA: National Council of Teachers of Mathematics.

Rowe, M.B. 1987. "Wait Time: Slowing Down May Be a Way of Speeding Up." *American Educator: The Professional Journal of the American Federation of Teachers.* 11 (1): 38–43, 47.

Supporting Classroom Talk

Teachers who encourage students' mathematical talk often find themselves talking less and listening more, spending more time speculating about students' comments and questions, and supporting students' mathematical thinking. Like them, you may find that your role shifts once your students engage in more discourse.

This section discusses some ways of supporting children's mathematical talk; there are others. These suggestions will meet some of your needs. But good mathematics discussions cannot always be planned; they tend to resist orchestration, may even seem spur-of-the-moment. We recommend that you seize opportunities to follow children's unexpected comments or questions—this often leads to excellent discussions.

The teachers we've worked with often comment on how difficult it is to plan a good discussion, and how important that planning is. They agree that being ready for an extended discussion or investigation is more than half the battle. If you're ready, you can pick up on subtle questions or less obvious ideas. If you aren't ready to listen to students, you will be less likely to hear what they are saying. Furthermore, if you aren't listening to students, they are not likely to listen to each other.

How Can Teachers Support Mathematical Talk?

There are many ways to support mathematical talk:

- Find engaging problems; suggest mathematical tasks that challenge each student's thinking.
- Provide various kinds of materials (Unifix cubes, beans,

17

balances, measuring equipment) for modeling or drawing mathematical situations and mathematical objects.
- Ask open questions that challenge and engage students' interest.
- Listen carefully, follow students' ideas closely, and allow time for everyone to think.
- Wonder about students' knowledge: children's mathematical thinking is complex.
- Support students' mathematics: build their number sense as well as their ability to connect representations and ideas.
- Do mathematics yourself: participate in a mathematical culture.
- Develop a mathematical community: a culture of inquiry should undergird a mathematics class.
- Expand and deepen children's communication; help them find their mathematical voice.

Find Engaging Problems

In order to talk about something, there has to be something worth talking about. Identifying a simple, compelling problem for students to begin work on is the central challenge in supporting their talk. David Hawkins suggests that relationships among teacher and students are best developed in the context of working on a shared endeavor. Grounding a discussion in a good problem is essential to having the talk make sense to all the participants.

Mathematics problems that engage students' imaginations needn't be elaborate or be embedded in complicated stories. They can be deceptively simple. (Marion Walter speaks directly to this in her essay "Curriculum Topics Through Problem Posing," included on page 141.)

In one second-grade classroom students were studying butterflies and had a monarch chrysalis in the classroom. They were intrigued by how many caterpillar legs there would be in the classroom if each student had a monarch caterpillar, so they figured it out. They went on to determine how many legs the butterflies that hatched from these chrysalises would have all together. Comparing the numbers of legs on butterflies and on caterpillars, they determined how many would be lost in the metamorphosis.

The students represented the problem in several ways. Jenny drew caterpillars and butterflies, counted all the legs on each, then compared the totals by finding the difference between them. Jamal found that

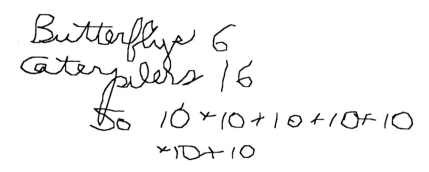

FIG. 2   Jamal's method.

each butterfly had six legs and each caterpillar had sixteen, so he added tens to get to the total of lost legs (see Figure 2). Sheila added sixteens to find the total of caterpillar legs and added sixes to find the total of butterfly legs (see Figure 3). She was intrigued that Jamal's method worked and spent a good deal of time doing the problem "Jamal's way." Both students were fascinated with the similarities and differences of their approaches.

Problems can also emerge from students' curiosity about their world. "Do all houses have windows that are the same size?" asked Joshua. This led first to speculation about how to measure windows. What would be the dimensions we'd need to compare them? What do we mean if we say that one window is bigger than another? Should we look at the perimeter of a window? The area? Children drew windows and cut out their pictures to compare them; then they measured windows in their houses for homework.

Section 4 of this book contains three classic mathematics problems that engage people of many ages. They are commercially available. "Strange Happenings" and "Pyramids" are interesting problems that can spark heated debates and long discussions. "Billiard Ball Trajectories" seems to work best with third graders and older children.

You'll have your own favorites: If you have six ice cream flavors and can combine them in double dip cones, how many different cones are possible? How much does it cost to raise a dog for a year? How many pencils does our class use in a year? What percentage of school

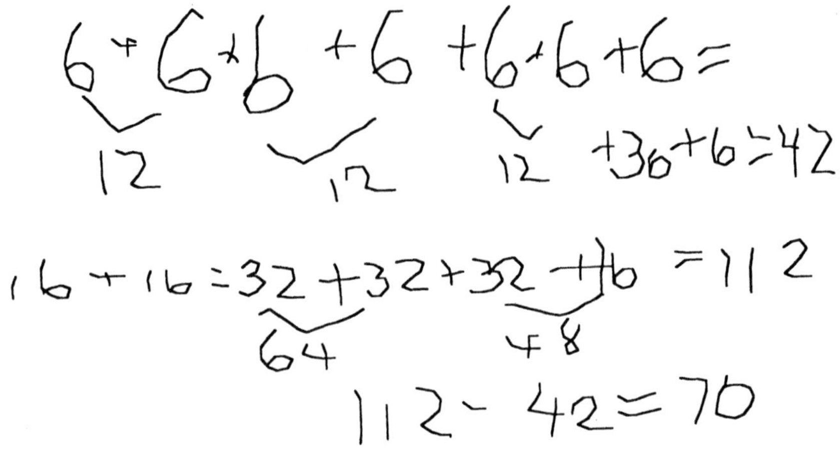

$$6 + 6 + 6 + 6 + 6 + 6 + 6 =$$
$$12 \qquad 12 \qquad 12 \quad +36 + 6 = 42$$

$$16 + 16 = 32 + 32 + 32 + 16 = 112$$
$$64 \qquad\qquad +8$$

$$112 - 42 = 70$$

FIG. 3   Sheila's method.

lunch is wasted daily? How many newspapers come from one tree? What things in the classroom come in pairs? Threes? How many ways can you find to make the number of today's date?

Problems that arise from real life often hold the most meaning for students. How many dogs does our class own? How many cats? What is the ratio? Is this true for the class next door? Is it true for the whole fourth grade? Is it true for the whole United States?

Many books include collections of interesting problems (see Resource List; you can also contact publishers directly to find others not listed there). Teaching magazines include suggestions. Pool your favorites with your colleagues so that everyone's repertoire is increased!

For inspiration, you can also turn to children's literature. For K–6 students, David Whitin and Sandra Wilde suggest many connections in *Read Any Good Math Lately?* (1992) and their recent *It's the Story That Counts* (1995). For primary students, there are suggestions in Marilyn Burns's and Stephanie Sheffield's *Math and Literature (K–3), Books One and Two* (1992). Teacher resource books such as the *Used Numbers* series (Dale Seymour 1990) and the California State Replacement Units will also be helpful.

Find ways of keeping track of problems that intrigue your students—you'll find excellent extensions and connections between and among them.

Provide Materials for Modeling and Drawing Problems

Making models or drawings of a mathematical situation allows students to explore many aspects of a problem simultaneously. When a problem is represented in different ways—three-dimensional models (clumps of beans, Unifix cubes, blocks), written or drawn symbols, and words—its richness becomes more apparent. Making connections between and among representations of a problem is an essential part of mathematics and is very satisfying.

Cecelia and Jamal worked on this problem: How many different ways can we make two-scoop ice cream cones out of four flavors? When they were done, they compared results. Cecelia claimed she could get four; Jamal said there were more. When their teacher asked how they could compare their methods, they were puzzled. Cecelia's paper had numbers written on it; Jamal's had pictures. "We didn't do the same thing," Jamal commented.

"You'll have to try to convince each other," said Ms. M.

A little while later, Jamal and Cecelia came back excitedly. "We see what we can do," they reported. "If we build ice cream cones with Unifix cubes or if we draw them or if we write the numbers down, it's all the same thing. We have all the same even though it looks different."

Seeing connections among representations is one of the important goals of mathematics. Representing and keeping track of information are important parts of what we want children to learn in their elementary school mathematics. If they can learn to record mathematical information and to work with what they record, they can more readily adapt to other methods as they are introduced.

Students represent information in many ways. They learn to keep track of their work as they *need* to do it. Just as they learn to draw by drawing and to write by writing, they learn to represent mathematics by doing it. Many of the most interesting mathematics investigations encourage a variety of representations.

Some representations may be graphic, some may be numeric, some may be geometric. Traditionally, we've taught students particular ways of recording and representing information in mathematics (often called algorithms or procedures), but this has not always worked. Remember finding the square root of a number with pencil and paper? You probably had to do it in high school, but was it worth the effort? Now it's easy to use a calculator to find a square root, and this shortcut does not interfere with your ability to understand what a square root is.

If we want students to make meaning from the mathematics they do, making their own representations of information, learning to keep track of the evolution of their own ideas, and talking about representations with their classmates are all important acts for them to undertake in the elementary grades. As students become more and more sophisticated, they seek elegant shortcuts in representing information and keeping records. Children refine their methods over time without sacrificing understanding.

But information is not tracked in a vacuum. If there is no reason to keep track of information, there is no reason to invent a method for doing so. When students deal with complex information, they find ways to organize it. If the information is rich and complicated, students have to deal with this real-life messiness. Sometimes an opportunity to report to another group raises issues of keeping track. Sometimes students do not know that they cannot rely on memory alone, especially when the data are complicated and messy.

Mathematics is a communication tool. Just as your students develop their own ways of representing information when they draw pictures or write stories, they must find their own representation methods with mathematical symbols. Transmitting conventional knowledge by showing the teacher's way of doing things does not work for many students. Just as we do not want our students to be passive writers or disinterested drawers, we do not want them to learn only top-down methods of recording mathematical information. You'll find that your students invent exciting ways to keep track of information and record their work. It is important that you not make suggestions; that way, they can develop their own methods.

To that end, materials must be always and easily available: calculators, crayons, sticky dots, Unifix cubes, blocks, Legos, and measuring tapes are all mathematical tools. If students feel ashamed to build models or use materials, we are giving them the wrong message about how mathematicians think and work. Inventing and enjoying many different mathematical representations is essential to developing a mathematical identity.

Ask Open Questions

Give your students open-ended questions to explore and investigate in small groups. These can be very simple. Peter Sullivan's essay "Improving the Quality of Learning by Asking 'Good' Questions," on page 129, is a good starting place for thinking about how to rephrase questions. Sullivan suggests turning ordinary computation examples around so that they have many answers. For instance, rather than posing the problem $3 + ? = 8$, he suggests framing it as, Two numbers add to eight. What might they be? or, How many combinations that make eight can you find that involve the number three?

With problems like these, students can compare their results with others'. Some students will find ways to order and generalize about solutions; others are content to find more than one solution. Each child gets more practice in doing and undoing combinations than they would if they were asked to solve one missing-addend problem. Comparing your results with your neighbor's is a wonderful stimulus to discussion and to learning. If there is only one right answer or one right method, talk tends to be shut off—there's really nothing to discuss.

For teachers, keeping a discussion alive involves finding a balance between teacher guidance and student talk. This creates some teaching dilemmas (see John Mason's "Tensions," on page 103). At first, students' engagement in investigations depends on the teacher's asking questions that catch their fancy and that promote mathematical exploration. Gradually those questions will come more often from the students themselves.

Some questions are *speculative* and may pique students' curiosity. They may present *challenges* and require students to test their own conjectures. Here are some examples:

- Do you think there are cases where that wouldn't work?
- Might there be numbers that have more than four factors?
- Do you think you would find the same patterns on another chart?

These spur some children to test their theories in order to convince others of their point of view. Speculating about counterexamples encourages children to explore some beginning forms of mathematical proof.

Questions can also direct students to *pay attention* to each other's ideas. You can directly convey that you expect children to listen to their classmates' ideas:

- Is Ariela's idea very different from yours, Joanne?
- Was anyone's idea about this problem like Sam's?
- What do you think about that, Jeremy?

If you expect students to listen to each other, you must be sure not to interpret everything they say and repeat it to the rest of the group. If every comment is filtered through you, there is little chance that your students will develop a conversation among themselves. Taking yourself out of the "interpreter's" role may be one of the hardest things to do, but it is often worth it.

Rather than rely on you to tell them whether they are correct, students can learn to rely more on their own ideas. Questions can help them to *move away from the external authority* of the teacher or the textbook:

- Does that seem right to you, George? How could you convince yourself?
- What would it take for you to be sure of your idea?

Your questions can also help students *use mathematical processes*. They can be invited to invent methods, make conjectures, and develop their own ideas:

- How might you approach this problem? Talk with your group to find two or three ways, and then let's share them.
- Do you have an idea you would like to try out?

And, of course, you can deepen students' awareness of the *connections* between what they are doing now in their investigations and other areas of mathematics:

- It this pattern anything like what you found when you explored those triangles?
- Does this remind you of any other mathematical investigations you've done?

Good questions that deepen children's thinking and investigation take many forms. It would be great if there were a surefire list of effective questions, but we all know that can't be—good questions are context specific. They usually arise in a moment of investigation or in the interaction between teacher and students or among students and often reflect *genuine curiosity* about the mathematics or about someone else's thinking. These effective questions are not, generally, yes-no questions or questions with one right answer. The important elements are that they be clear, that they fit the mathematical situation, and that they be aimed at clarifying or extending students' thinking.

Listen Carefully

Nothing is more important than YOU: listening to students carefully, wanting to hear many different ideas, showing that your students have something to say that's worth hearing. You can collect students' ideas and help them become more articulate and more aware of one another's ideas as well. If you listen to students' ideas supportively, they are likely to express more ideas the next time.

Vivian Paley, in her essay "On Listening to What the Children Say" (page 113), writes of her experiences with young children. She details how she came to use a tape recorder as part of "a daily search for the child's point of view." Her sensitivity to children's meanings has to reach across the apparent gulf between adult logic and the logic of young children; to do this she listens carefully and wholeheartedly to students.

It is important that all of us learn to listen more. Unfortunately, most of our training has been in how to present information, to talk, and to direct children's attention. It is high time we also address the issue of listening closely to *their* talk.

You can practice listening closely by asking your colleagues to do mathematics problems and describe their strategies to you. Listen openly to their approaches and ask questions when you can't follow or need to learn more about their reasons. You might also practice listening by instigating a five-minute period of silence (yours, not your students') during a class discussion. Nodding, saying "oh," and literally repeating a student's words encourage them to add to what they've said. Active listening is important, and it can be done in mathematics classrooms.

Listening carefully may involve reflecting students' ideas back to them; it may involve asking them to expand their comments because you don't quite understand what they're saying. "Let me see if I understand. You think that . . ." is one way to check a child's meaning.

Repeating a student's words but rephrasing them is a source of some concern. Over and over teachers take student ideas and make them into something tidier or more efficient. Although this may be done with the best of motives, it raises serious questions. One teacher who was concerned about putting words into her students' mouths decided that she rephrased their ideas and patted their words into shape because she wanted them to seem smarter. She came to believe that by doing this she was preventing students from having their own voices. After working for a year to stop it, she was able to allow students their own voices and their own vocabularies in her classroom. And she also found that more students participated in discussions and talked more honestly and in more depth about their own ideas and their own ways of seeing things. Her struggle to listen bore fruit.

Mary Budd Rowe, a science educator, has done research for years about discussions in science classes. She has found (Rowe 1987) that increasing a pause after a question (the teacher's "wait time") increases participation and involvement as well as the quality of students' responses. Surprisingly, it appears that a wait of only three seconds facilitates significant changes in student involvement. Surely it's worth three seconds to encourage more students to talk!

There are some repercussions to spending more time listening to students. First, you will need to balance interactions in ways different from some of the ones you use now. Second, you may wish to record classroom sessions so that you can learn more about what happens there. Third, and most important, you may find that your students' ideas and questions are so compelling that you begin to shift your curriculum.

Listening closely to students may raise new questions about their understanding of mathematics. These, in turn, may raise questions about teaching and learning mathematics.

Wonder About Students' Knowledge

When you respond with curiosity and interest, your students feel their ideas are interesting and valuable, and they will talk more, thus rewarding you with new information about their thinking.

Don't you wonder what your students really think about odd versus even numbers? Do you understand what sense they make of regrouping in subtraction? What does your class think about the hundred board or the number line?

There are times when we become researchers in the classroom—when our students say things we do not expect and we follow that reasoning in many directions. We can't do this all the time, but when we do we show our students that mathematics and mathematical ideas are interesting and worth understanding.

"Tell me everything you can about these," says Ms. A to her third-grade class at the beginning of the year. The children are sitting in a circle on the rug. She opens her hands and shows them two numeral 2's and two numeral 3's (see Figure 4). She waits.

Aisha: There are twos and threes.
Paul: I see two twos and two threes.
Elie: There's a three for every two and a two for every three.
Ms. A: Yes, there's one for each one.
Neelie: If you make them add up, you get ten.
Ken: If you make them all double, you get twenty-two and thirty-three.
Ms. A: Would you show your idea on the board so we can all see? (Ken goes to the board and draws Figure 5.) Thank you.
Ham: I think you can make two hundred and twenty-three and three, too.
Ms. A: Are there other numbers we can make?
Several students: Three hundred and twenty-two and three.
Several students: Twenty-three and twenty-three.
Jeremy: There is three thousand two hundred and twenty-three if you put them all in the same number.
Su-Mei: If you say there are two twos then you say there are four. If you say there are two threes then you say there are six. So it's kind of like four and six in disguise.

Students continue exploring the other ways the numerals can be combined to make "disguised" numbers. It lasts for twenty minutes, much to Ms. A's surprise.

With one open-ended question, Ms. A learned a great deal in a short time. She felt that these third-grade students displayed flexibility in thinking about numerals. She hadn't known what to expect when

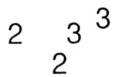

FIG. 4   Ms. A's twos and threes.

she started, but she wanted her students to have a chance to do something with them. She had not wanted to prejudge what they were likely to know and express.

On reflection, Ms. A concluded that many students were interested in exploring ways of representing different numbers, that Sue-Mei enjoyed looking beneath the surface of a problem, and that Jeremy was able to see and create numbers well into the thousands. After this session she made some notes and decided to pursue the question throughout the school year, recording children's observations at different times. We can all become classroom researchers like this, exploring the many ways our students understand mathematics and the approaches that seem to help them best.

Support Students' Mathematics

Develop Number Sense

"Number sense" seems deceptively obvious. You have probably had students who did not seem to have number sense, as well as those who seemed to have a lot. We have all felt this in our own lives as well. In our own mathematics there were times when we felt we had a good sense of what we were doing, and other times when we did not.

A sense of number is developed by experience—exploring, manipulating, playing, posing questions, and finding patterns. Beyond that, students with a powerful sense of number have intuitions about how numbers are constructed. They often think of numbers as landmarks in our base-ten system.

Many school-age students have learned not to trust their intuitions about how numbers behave. They no longer trust their sense of what

$$22 \quad 33$$

FIG. 5   *Ken's results.*

might be important about 100, or how a number series like 4, 8, 12, 16 is constructed. Overemphasizing rote procedures may cause students to suspend their common sense about numbers (at least while they are in school).

Students may become passive in mathematics class, waiting for a teacher to tell them what to do. They may learn to pay attention for long enough to find out what to do and how to do it, and then apply those procedures to each of the problems assigned. Although this may be a valuable coping strategy, it is not a good way to investigate or explore mathematics; certainly it is not the way to develop mathematical power.

To break this cycle, we need to encourage students to make sense of whatever they do. They must be given problems that pique their interest in numbers. For example, many students are interested in the number 100. They become engaged in mathematical exploration when given the problem shown in Figure 6.

The many solutions create patterns to explore. As students work in small groups and then as a class to find as many solutions as possible, a new kind of thinking may emerge. What patterns do they see? How many solutions do they find? A constant emphasis on creating meaning, making sense, and evaluating results helps an investigation like this.

Presenting problems that have many correct or reasonable solutions is only one approach to developing number sense. It's also important to pay attention to the relative size or location of numbers (e.g., 101 is not much more than 98; 100 is a lot closer to 10 than to 1000). Students can begin to sharpen their sense of whether a number is closer to one or another landmark. Is 1¾ closer to 1 or 2? Is 9 closer to 5 or 10? Is 23 closer to 25 or 20? Can you name two numbers between 10

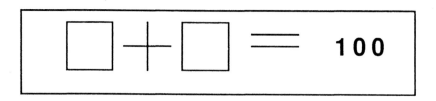

FIG. 6   Problem for mathematical exploration.

and 30? Which one of those is closer to 30? How can you tell? Is 564 closest to a fourth, a half, or three-fourths of the way between 500 and 600?

Students can develop flexibility by looking at the structure of an individual number (24 can be constructed of two tens and four ones, 24 is 10 more than 14, half of 24 is 12, three eights equal 24, etc.). We don't want students to think about a number as its individual digits but to keep a sense of how it is constructed *as a whole*.

Questions like "How many ways can you make 12?" encourage students to compose and decompose numbers with facility. As they become more practiced, asking them to make as many numbers as possible using four operations and four digits (1, 2, 3, 4) becomes an engaging exercise.

A sense of approximation helps us judge the reasonableness of results. If we add 19 and 22, will the answer be closer to 40 or 50? What are some useful ways to think about this? If we add 1¾ and 2½, will the answer be more or less or equal to 3? 4? Questions such as these can be asked whenever students are working.

Above all, the urge to find an unknown or solve a problem is important. There is a joy in predicting from the known to the unknown, a joy in asking questions to try to make sense of number and quantity. We want to be sure to develop and treasure that urge in all our students.

Find Patterns

Finding patterns is at the heart of learning complex information. When Jill begins to count, she creates her own "rules" for the number system.

The patterns she finds can be seen when she counts: "Twenty-eight, twenty-nine, twenty-ten, twenty-'leven." Although her last two responses are considered "mistakes" in many school settings, they indicate that she knows a great deal about number patterns, particularly about place value. Jill knows that ten comes after nine, the decade name comes before the unit name, and number names go in the same order all the time. She has also uncovered an extremely powerful pattern: you can reuse the counting numbers and recombine them to create the names of bigger and bigger numbers.

Children often make grammatical errors that make their pattern-finding skills more evident to us. Many children say *brang* or *bringed* at some point in their language learning—as in, I brang my lunchbox to school—showing strong knowledge of the patterns of *regular* verb forms and a good predictive ability. When a student makes this kind of "logical" mistake with words and word forms, we don't worry much about it, since we assume that the child will indeed learn to speak correctly. We don't tend to make the same assumptions about mathematical "errors," although we should.

Many mathematicians consider mathematics to be the science of patterns (Steen 1988). One core activity of mathematics is finding and describing patterns, extending them, and testing them to see whether they hold true under a variety of conditions. The formula for finding the circumference of a circle ($C = \pi d$) must have begun to emerge as someone noticed the pattern that the circumference seemed always to be a little more than three times the diameter. That conjecture was explored and tested, further and further refined, and evolved into the formula as we know it. It allows us to know how much fencing will surround a small round garden, what size piece of wood to cut for a table top, how much rickrack to buy to outline a circle on a class quilt.

Patterns lie at the heart of prediction. Number patterns allow us to count to the next number—all the way to infinity. If we know that two tens is 20, three tens are 30, then we may be able to see that nine tens are likely to be 90—and perhaps that twelve tens make 120.

Knowing patterns lets me figure out $\$6.99 \times 7$ by rounding to $\$7$, figuring that $7 \times 7 = 49$, and taking off the "extra pennies" I put there when I rounded to get $\$48.93$. Every computational shortcut is the result of having found a pattern. Having discovered that order doesn't matter when adding whole numbers allows us to be able to take a long column of numbers and find combinations that add to ten.

First a child *sees* a pattern, then *talks about it*, then begins to see *whether* it is always true, then tries to explore *why* it is the way it is. These steps should be the basis of much classroom mathematical activity.

These second-grade students have skip-counted by twos on a hundred board, and are looking at what they've marked.

Ms. D: What can you tell me about these numbers?

Jen: They are all in the same places but up one.

Ms. D: Say a little more about that.

Jen: When you go up the numbers go like from four to fourteen to twenty-four to thirty-four. The front number goes up one.

Mandy: They're all in the same places. Up from two, up from four.

Warren: And you go every other, every other. Like not these [*points to the column that ends in ones*], these [*twos*] are marked, not these [*threes*], the next ones are marked [*fours*], not these [*fives*] . . .

Ms. D: Would this be true if we went higher than a hundred?

Pearl: No, because a hundred is different.

Bets: No! I mean yes, because it's the same only with a hundred in front.

This teacher is doing a skillful job of extending the children's observations and ideas.

Here are some techniques you can use when working with patterns:

1. *Describe a pattern in words:* Putting a pattern into words that another person can understand is the first step in recording that pattern.

2. *Record a pattern in informal language:* Writing down students' patterns allows them to come back to their observations and conjectures and test them later. Some teachers record students' ideas on large chart paper that the students can refer to as they test the patterns they find.

3. *Ask students to write and draw their patterns:* After students have become fairly fluent in *talking* patterns, encourage them to find ways to draw and write their ideas. Working in pairs may make this easier.

4. *Test and make predictions:* As students identify patterns, encourage them to test patterns to see whether they always

hold up. Can it be used to predict other occurrences of the number? Although this may be hard for young students, ask them *why* a pattern might work. Their answers may surprise you.

5. *Use your curiosity to inspire students:* Encourage your students by modeling your own interest in patterns and in finding patterns that can be used for predictions. When a student finds an unusual or unexpected pattern, test it and enjoy it. There are always new patterns to be seen, described, and analyzed.

Connect Symbols and Words

Individuals and communities construct written symbols and spoken words to reflect their experiences. This took time historically, and still does. Our students need many, many experiences with number, space, and data before the conventional mathematical symbols will fit naturally into situations.

As an example, think of $+$. This seems simple to us as adults, but it is not such a simple symbol for our students to learn. Mathematically, this written symbol can stand for different things. It sometimes stands for an operation (addition) but also represents a relationship (more than). In $3 + 5 = 8$ we may be saying, Three plus five equals eight, but we may also be saying, Three and five more are eight. Depending on the context of the problem, the same symbol signifies different actions or relationships: $3 + 5 = ?$ can be read as $3 + 5$ is what? or what is the equivalent of 3 and 5 more? or 3 and 5 make what? or what number is five more than three?

Before we can expect our students to use abstract terms with precision, we must make sure they have experienced relevant situations. This is best done by helping them explore and make sense of many problem situations.

If teachers use correct mathematical terms, students learn those correct terms. If we *also* use students' informal language, we help students construct appropriate concepts and match them with language. It may be most effective to proceed on both fronts simultaneously, using students' own language and conventional mathematical terminology in the same situations *without making an issue of it.*

If we treat mathematical conventions as *laws,* we convey the wrong message. Conventional symbols and words are important, but they are based on centuries of negotiation. They represent the high end of specification and precision, but they should not supplant informal vocabulary too quickly.

After all, if you can tell what a student means when writing or talking, that student has effectively communicated his or her ideas regardless of the precision of the terminology. Remember that language conventions have been constructed by people and that people agree on meanings. Allow yourself and your students some flexibility here—if we teach words more than we support ideas, we end up with mastery of neither.

Do Mathematics Yourself

We know from our work on the Talking Mathematics project that doing mathematics and reflecting on it are essential components in developing better mathematics teachers. It is exciting to have your own mathematical understanding grow. For instance, listen to this fourth-grade teacher:

> I have been doing some reading about square, triangular, and pentagonal numbers. These baffled but fascinated me during the seminar. I kept thinking that the concept was just too big and that's why I couldn't get it. I'm not sure now that the "bigness" was really the stumbling block. Part of my difficulty was that even with my raised consciousness I was still holding on to a very limited definition of math. (I still separate my definition from my understanding.)

Teachers who have the opportunity to explore mathematics with colleagues report a new awareness of the power of the group in doing mathematics. One commented:

> I gained a lot of insight into my learning in a group and how helpful a group can be to me. I learned that I very much need and want manipulatives nearby when I'm trying to understand something. (I say nearby because then even if I'm not using them in any given moment, someone else might be and that might give me ideas, and also sometimes my just looking at manipulatives gives me ideas.) I learned that concrete is not less sophisticated than abstract:

> I think instead it has to do with learning and something to do with experience with a problem and lots to do with how someone thinks.

This teacher's sense of the role of the group is different from the one many of us got in mathematics classes. Rather than seeing classmates as a support, many of us learned they were a source of competition, correction, and challenge. Although a mathematical community may represent those aspects of group membership, it is also important to understand the role of the group in constructing shared understanding. Unless one has participated in such a group, it may remain a mystery.

Your own mathematics may be somewhat spotty. In the last ten years more mathematicians and mathematics educators have begun to write about doing mathematics. There are many valuable and interesting books on the market. Perhaps the most helpful are those that describe the mathematical experience, such as Philip Davis and Reuben Hersh's *The Mathematical Experience* (1981) and Lynn Steen's *On the Shoulders of Giants* (1990). Reading these books (or, for many of us, dipping into them) allows us to see that there is a good deal more flexibility in this field than our own educations led us to believe.

If you want to find a mathematical community, you might encourage your staff developer or mathematics coordinator to offer a long-term workshop that is not about looking for classroom activities (there are plenty of those) but that focuses on the group members' professional growth in doing mathematics. There are also supportive classes in colleges and universities, or you may be able to form a group of teachers who want to do ongoing classroom research.

Helpful resources range from conferences to university courses to your colleagues. If all of those are inappropriate to your situation, consider doing mathematics with your students. Perhaps once a month, try a problem that you've never done before, and do it with the students. You might invite a neighboring class to join you, so that you can work in an even larger community. (That way, too, you would be working with a colleague.)

However it happens, we encourage you to join with others to make sense of the large and growing arena of mathematics. As your own sense of mathematics becomes more sturdy, you will find yourself more open to thinking about your students' mathematical understanding. Although it may seem hard to believe, you have nothing to lose.

Develop a Mathematical Community

This takes time. Our students never seem to "get it" in the same way at the same time. Janine doesn't understand that a fraction represents parts of a whole; Leroy doesn't understand that mixed numbers can be represented as fractions. When Susan writes $\frac{9}{8}$ she means the same thing as when she writes $\frac{8}{9}$. Given an eight-slice pizza, Kelly doesn't always know how many pieces she would get if she took $\frac{5}{8}$ of it.

Students come to school with knowledge about numbers. At home they have counted and used (or at least played with) money. They talk about time and measurement. They hear adults and older children talk about numerical concepts when they make change, find differences, or estimate quantities.

We know that these students didn't begin to walk at the same time; they didn't talk at the same time. Nevertheless, we do seem to expect them to learn mathematics at the same time and in the same way, even though we know that they won't. This conundrum puts us in a difficult position. We want our students to learn the same material from the same exposure; yet we know from our own evidence that students' ideas are very different.

Students build ideas based on prior experiences, the meanings they make of a situation, their knowledge about a topic, the connections they make to other areas, and more. Ideas are constructed, developed, matched with language, stored, retrieved. Sense is made of them, then lost, then regained. In order to build solid mathematical concepts, students need experience with many different models over time. Just as they develop spoken and written language facility along different timetables, they construct mathematical ideas at very different rates.

We can capitalize on having such diversity in the classroom if we can support our students in a mathematical community where they compare, discuss, and debate their work. How many cookies do we each get if there are four of us and six cookies? Aisha says there will be one and a half; Shaun says there will be one and a couple of pieces; Jo says we'll each get six pieces. Who is right? Are we all talking about the same thing? How can we decide? If there were no differences there would be nothing to talk about, but since their answers seem different, there is a good opportunity to explore and compare. Learning to talk about what she does and thinks, comparing and contrasting her methods with those of others, and working with others to explore both similarities and differences allow a student to validate her own methods, to develop her understanding, and to find her own mathematical voice.

Wouldn't it be convenient if students "got it" along with our lesson plans! When the Aha! strikes or the light bulb is turned on and illuminates a student's understanding, we sometimes allow ourselves to think that he really *does* understand for good and always. We are disappointed when that understanding is ephemeral, gone the next day.

We need to remember what happens when we try to learn something new and fairly abstract—chemistry, perhaps, or a new language, or playing a musical instrument. At first we learn some basics, only to realize in a day or two that we didn't really anchor that learning in experience; it seems to vanish. If we learn in a community, we experience the kind of talk that anchors knowledge and builds a foundation that can support our further learning. The same is true of children.

Although many students can manipulate symbols for a short time after a unit is taught, there is plenty of evidence that they may not have mastered the basic concepts (just ask the teachers in the next grade!). Traditionally, mathematics teachers have been taught to wean students onto written symbols very quickly, so we sometimes teach procedures instead of emphasizing conceptual understanding. This has limited our ability to see understanding grow among a whole class, and it surely limits the development of mathematical community in our classrooms.

Expand and Deepen Children's Communication

Shared talk is at the heart of many communities. In a mathematical community, students use language to communicate mathematical ideas. Their talk expresses, clarifies, or conveys their observations or questions. In a community, students are not afraid to take risks or to make mistakes; the community recognizes error as a part of contributing to collective knowledge.

Often, we work to help students become active listeners so that each member of a group may speak more frequently and in greater depth. Students who have never before been expected to participate in mathematical discourse may need support in order to contribute. Asking students to discuss a problem or idea in a small group before reporting to the large group can help everyone participate more. When the small group shares its work with everyone, all students know they have made contributions to the class' knowledge base.

Working with someone else is a way of opening up everyone's thought processes. A mathematical community shares their referents and their experiences. When they talk directly with each other, they are sharing in the construction of community as well as building mathematical knowledge.

You can support a sense of community by valuing appropriate contributions, by keeping track of what investigations are being pursued, and by helping students refer to each other's ideas. Naming patterns after their inventors, reading from the observations that groups make, and encouraging students to post their ideas for everyone to share will make a difference. You will be the community historian; you can create a sense of a shared past.

Further, though, you can help your students develop a kind of interdependence that allows them to see that the whole is greater than the sum of its parts. Each student contributes to everyone's knowledge and understanding. Participating in that kind of mathematical culture is exceptionally satisfying.

Developing a mathematical community is not easy, however. You may find that new questions about teaching emerge just as quickly as you try new things. Dilemmas are constantly resurfacing, and they need to be addressed.

- How do I know when to tell and when not to tell?
- When should I introduce "correct" mathematical language and symbols?
- Which ideas should I pursue in depth?
- How much should I insist that all students participate in discussions? Are some students just quiet?

As you strive to develop your understanding of your students' mathematics, there will be times when you reinvent some aspects of your teaching. You may find that you want to explore your pedagogy in more depth. This is an emerging field, and there are many others who are engaged in that exploration with you. Just as your students need to feel a sense of community, you do too. Finding even one person to share ideas with is worthwhile; finding more than one is bounty.

References

Burns, M. 1992. *Math and Literature (K-3)*. Book 1. Sausalito, CA: The Math Solution Publications. Distributed by Cuisenaire.

Davis, P. J. & R. Hersh. 1981. *The Mathematical Experience*. Boston, MA: Houghton Mifflin.

Rowe, M. B. 1987. "Wait Time: Slowing Down May Be a Way of Speeding Up." *American Educator: The Professional Journal of the American Federation of Teachers* 11(1):38–43, 47.

Sheffield, S. 1992. *Math and Literature (K-3)*. Book 2. Sausalito, CA: The Math Solution Publications. Distributed by Cuisenaire.

Steen, L. A. 1988. "The Science of Patterns." *Science* 240 (4852): 611–16.

———, ed. 1990. *On the Shoulders of Giants: New Approaches to Numeracy*. Washington, DC: Mathematical Sciences Education Board.

Whitin, D. & S. Wilde. 1992. *Read Any Good Math Lately? Children's Books for Mathematical Learning, K–6*. Portsmouth, NH: Heinemann.

———. 1995. *It's the Story That Counts: More Children's Books for Mathematical Learning, K–6*. Portsmouth, NH: Heinemann.

Readings

Introduction

The essays we have included are direct recommendations from the teachers who took part in the Talking Mathematics project. Some focus on doing and reflecting on mathematics; some focus on children's learning and thinking; some focus on overall teaching issues.

Many of these essays were written quite some time ago; they form a significant part of the teaching literature focused on mathematics and science. Each of these writers has an important voice that we hope will speak directly to you. Eleanor Duckworth, Vivian Paley, Marion Walter, and David Hawkins offer strong reflections on children's thinking and are also important teacher educators. This shared reference base will allow you to talk a kind of "family shorthand" with like-minded teachers.

These authors discuss many interesting problems, and we recommend you take time to try some of them with your students. Jeannie Billington's very detailed presentation of what happened when her students did the handshake problem gives much to think about. Peter Sullivan's work shows how to present "ordinary" mathematics questions in open-ended ways. It has helped many teachers rethink their questioning techniques without having to rethink the entire curriculum.

Joan Countryman's chapter on writing in mathematics is a good introduction to the kinds of writing that can be used in mathematics. If we think of mathematics as communication, writing is as much a part of that process as model building or talking is. Her insights about change are very helpful.

And John Mason's open discussion about the dilemmas and difficulties of deciding how to teach is uniquely reassuring to the many teachers who feel that their lack of certainty shows only that they are indecisive. Mason gives a very different interpretation.

These readings have inspired some teachers, moved others, and opened new doors for many. We hope they will do the same for you.

41

How many handshakes are possible among four people? Six people? Twenty people?

The "Handshake Problem" is a straightforward, classic mathematics problem. It can be approached in a variety of ways and encourages many different styles of representing information. Because the numbers quickly grow too large to keep track of easily, they need to be captured in some kind of model to be manipulated and understood.

This essay describes the approaches children age six to fifteen have taken to the "Handshake Problem," along with samples of their work. (The original collection of artwork was richer than appears here—we have been able to include only selections.) The children's excitement as they find ways to work with complicated problems is well conveyed.

This problem elicits a rich assortment of solution strategies. Surprisingly, children's and adults' representations are often similar. You may want to compare some of the representations provided here and figure out the students' thinking.

Levels of Knowing 2: "The Handshake"*

Jeannie Billington and Patricia Evans

> *In the end it took me 3 hours, the answer was*
> *Get the two top numbers like a 100 99*
> *times them, get your answer and half it*
> *and there is the result.*
>
> THE END
> BY DEAN (age 10)

Dean's written words in no way convey the sheer joy and delight he expressed at the time of his discovery. The surge of excitement which he experienced is an important part of knowing. What happened at that moment of discovery? What mental processes were taking place? What did he see with his inner eye?

Dean had been working on a variation of the following problem:

> There were seven people at a party. If everyone shook hands with everyone else once and once only, how many handshakes would there be?

The *handshake problem* is a very simple one and can be used at many different levels, from a purely practical problem for young children through to generalising and proving the results for *n* people. We have

* Originally published in *Mathematics Teaching* 120 (September 1987): 12–18.

worked on the problem with many children whose ages range from 6 to 15.

Factors Influencing the Children's Success

Children demonstrated through the *handshake problem* several levels of knowing. Their ability to do so was influenced by three external variables:

- The nature and presentation of the problem; a tangible aspect
- The general strategies used by the children; a less tangible aspect
- The role of the teacher

The Nature and Presentation of the Problem

The handshake problem appeared to enable children to illustrate their ability to get an answer, find a rule and know why the rule works. There were those children who found an answer and were convinced, with varying levels of confidence, that their answer was right! Some children, not content with finding an answer, went on to search for a rule which would work for any number of people shaking hands. There were interesting levels of sophistication in the development of the rule. Ultimately there were those children who could see why the rule worked. We do not want to imply that there are cut-and-dried stages of knowing. The take-half problem (Billington and Evans 1986) for example, does not have the same 'get an answer—find a rule' stage as the handshake problem.

General Strategies Used by the Children

We were intrigued by the general strategies the children used. The Cockcroft Report describes general strategies as 'procedures which guide the choice of which skills to use or what knowledge to draw upon at each stage in the course of solving a problem or carrying out an investigation. They enable a problem to be approached with confidence and with the expectation that a solution will be possible.' There was evidence, at different levels of the handshake problem, of children's ability to:

- process information and 'own' the problem
- make predictions and test them
- symbolise
- tabulate
- illustrate their mental pictures and/or physical actions by diagrams
- search for and investigate patterns
- see connections
- generalise
- establish a proof

It seemed that a combination of some of these abilities enabled the children to find solutions.

The Role of the Teacher

The role of the teacher is crucial in the 'enabling.' We are convinced that some, if not all, of the general strategies listed above are natural to children and should be developed not taught. Children need to know that their ideas are not only acceptable but encouraged. Allowing time and space for children to develop and test their own predictions is essential.

We have recorded the children's work under the following headings: getting an answer; finding a rule; and knowing why the rule works. We have tried to demonstrate the strategies that the children are using. The work is mainly of two age groups: second-year juniors and fourth-year secondary.

The children were introduced to the problem verbally. They were encouraged to work collaboratively, sharing and developing their own ideas and those of others. Although the younger children worked collaboratively, they tended to write up their solutions individually and in their own time. The older children wrote group solutions. They were expected from the beginning to generalise the situation, e.g., 'How many handshakes for seven people, twenty-seven people, 'n' number of people?'

Getting an Answer

PROCESSING INFORMATION AND 'OWNING' THE PROBLEM The children needed to clarify certain points. The younger children, in particular, asked the following types of questions:

What's a handshake?
Do you have to shake hands with everybody?
Do you shake hands with yourself?
Can you shake hands more than once?
If I shake hands with Marlon is that one handshake or two?

Once the boundaries of the problem were clearly defined, they began to make predictions. The older children, plus a few younger ones, made predictions immediately (see Figure A).

We did not, at this stage, ask the children to describe the problem in their own words. However, we are including some of the children's descriptions of the problem, taken from their written solutions. It is interesting to see how individuals or groups interpreted the problem.

Daniel's 'text-book' description of the problem was very sophisticated. He was quick, when the problem was first posed, to establish the basic parameters by asking a few very pertinent questions. His solution and extension of the problem were more elaborate than those of any other child in his age group. Martha found it necessary to weave a story around the problem and to use real characters. It was Hoan's first attempt at problem solving. Although successful, she was the only child who did not symbolise or use diagrams. She was new to the school and we presume had not been encouraged to 'problem solve' before. We always encourage our children to use apparatus or draw diagrams to help them. The older children's descriptions were, as expected, much more advanced.

MAKING AND TESTING THEIR PREDICTIONS   Many 'hunches' were plucked out of the air as being immediate solutions. The older children tended to use algebraic expressions. Some obvious predictions were made. We heard:

'It's n^2.'
'It's 2n.'
'8!'
'It's 8×8.'
'It's 8×2.'
'8×7.'
'It's 64.'
'It's 16.'
'56!'

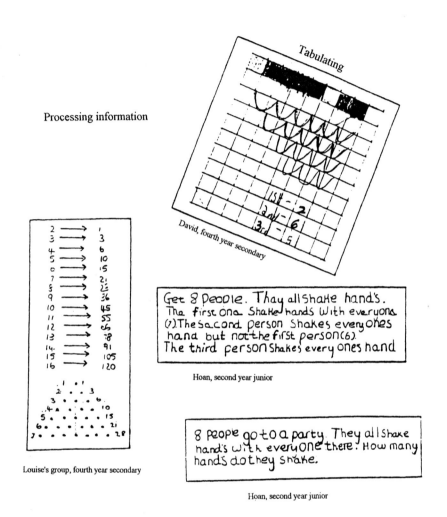

Processing information

Tabulating

David, fourth year secondary

Get 8 People. Thay all Shake hand's. Tha first ona Shake hands With everyona (7). The Sacond person Shakes every ones hand but not the first person (6). The third person Shakes every ones hand

Hoan, second year junior

Louise's group, fourth year secondary

8 People go to a party. They all Shake hand's with every one there? How many hands do they Shake.

Hoan, second year junior

FIG. A   *Getting an answer.*

A period of intense activity followed. The 'hunches' seemed to have been forgotten amidst this activity, but the children returned to them once they had reached the stage of finding a rule.

SYMBOLISING   The children surprised us by using a wide variety of symbols. They included combinations of the following: colour, dots, letters of the alphabet, names, numbers, objects (e.g. Unifix), 'pin' people and the children themselves.

TABULATING   The symbolising seemed to develop into tabulating. There were two types of tabulation: one related to solving the first part of the problem, e.g., eight people at a party, and the other related to extending the problem to other numbers of people. It was interesting to observe those children who included one person—nil handshakes. Daniel was the only second-year junior child to explore beyond the first part of the problem. He did so of his own accord. However, he was not prepared to investigate further than producing his table (see Figure B).

ILLUSTRATING THEIR MENTAL PICTURES AND/OR PHYSICAL ACTIONS WITH DIAGRAMS   The majority of younger children needed to solve the problem physically. They either arranged themselves in groups and actually shook hands or they used real objects such as Unifix. Some of these younger children began to work out the problem using themselves but found the task frustrating because a few would not stand still. They reverted to using objects or drawing diagrams. The older children tended to visualise the problem mentally from the start, and depicted their mental images on paper.

We were astounded, at first, by the similarity between the diagrams drawn by the younger and older children. However, we realised on reflection that certain problems lend themselves to the use of certain diagrams, such as networks and mappings, which both appeared. The younger children tended to reinforce their diagrams with colours and names. These factors generally were absent from the older children's work.

Daniel, once again, was the only junior child to use a 'graph.'

SEARCHING FOR AND INVESTIGATING PATTERNS   Through the development of the diagrams, patterns began to emerge. Most children, regardless of age, spotted the consecutive number pattern. For the younger ones, this was as far as they were prepared to go. They were able to explain, when questioned, that with 19 people, for example, there would be 18 + 17 + 16 + 15 . . . handshakes. They were rather pleased with themselves and had had enough for one day. The older children went on to investigate different numbers of people. Several of them spotted the triangular number pattern but none of them investigated the differ-

1 person – 0	handshakes	
2 people – 1	handshake	
3 people – 3	handshakes	
4 people – 6	handshakes	
5 people – 10	handshakes	
6 people – 15	handshakes	
7 people – 21	handshakes	
8 people – 28	handshakes	
9 people – 36	handshakes	
10 people – 45	handshakes	

FIG. B   Daniel's table.

ences between the triangular numbers. They used other methods to find a rule and proof. (This is particularly interesting when most mathematical textbooks emphasize these differences.)

One very able second-year junior child, Ruth, did use differences to establish a rule. Her work is included under the 'Finding a Rule' section.

All the children who persevered with the problem found an answer to the first part of it. Using real objects or their mathematical diagrams, they were able to convince themselves and others of the 'correctness' of their answers. This gave them a great sense of satisfaction and creativity. They could do it! For some of the older children it had taken a matter of minutes. For others it had been a much longer, and in some cases, arduous task. Marlon, for example, needed to reinforce his understanding of the problem by explaining his solution to his friends and his class teacher, by using unifix, before it really clicked. As a child who can hardly read or write, he was very proud of his final diagram. All of the children had a sense of achievement, to a lesser or greater degree depending on how tortuous their route had been and how secure they were in knowing that they were right.

Finding a Rule

GENERALISING The confidence gained from finding the 'correct' answer to the first part of the problem gave some children the incentive to generalise and make predictions for other numbers and situations. There were various levels of sophistication in their attempts to do so. These levels can be categorised as follows:

- Seeing the consecutive number pattern
- Seeing the triangular number pattern
- Finding a logical explanation
- Finding an algebraic explanation

Most children spotted the consecutive number pattern, but there were differences in the degree of confidence shown by children in applying this understanding to other numbers. When Shaun, age 8, was asked if it would work for any number, he suggested:

S: Well get them all in a row—it doesn't matter how big, and the person at the top goes down the row shaking hands. Well, he has to do the number of people less one because he can't shake hands with himself. Then he goes away from the room and the next person gets going. He can't have done it before with anyone otherwise he'd have to get out of line. So his number of handshakes is one less than the first one. If you keep it up you will be left with only one person who hasn't got anyone else and you are finished.
T: Would it work for even one million? [very stupid question]

S: Well I don't know. I don't think so.

T: Why? You said it would work for all numbers.

S: Well the line would be too long and people would get fed up waiting for a shake.

Shaun knew the method would work but had qualms about people getting bored. The fourteen-year olds did not have this problem. Their certainty showed itself in the following formula:

n people $= (n - 1) + (n - 2) + (n - 3) + (n - 4) + (n - 5) + (n - 6) + (n - 7) \ldots$
until $n - (n - 1)$

Some children spotted the triangular number pattern:

1 person—0 handshakes
2 people—1 handshake
3 people—3 handshakes
4 people—6 handshakes

However, this was not particularly helpful in finding the ultimate formula. The older children realised this and the problem began to change. It became 'how do you find the sum of the first n natural numbers?' A lull followed this change. The lull was vital. Children began to try out ideas and play with them. At this stage it was very important to give them time and space. In short they were 'stuck,' and it was difficult to watch and wait without interfering. If they were to reach their own level of knowing, it was important to allow them to select their own route. There are times when it is necessary to intervene, but this was not one of them. It took Dean (age 10) three hours. His class had been doing a project on communication. They had been studying British Telecom services. The handshake problem became the 'houses and cables' problem. Dean was fascinated by the patterns that emerged and had worked hard to determine the number of cables needed for 200 homes. He eventually found a logical solution. He was thrilled. The fourteen-year-olds, after playing with summing numbers and trying out

FIG. C   Many processes are illustrated.

rules, generally came back to the structure of the problem itself, and solutions began to emerge (see Figure C). Sarah's group generated:

the rule $\dfrac{n^2 - n}{2}$ *or* $\dfrac{n(n-1)}{2}$
both of these work

Stephen's group formulated:

We derived two rules:

$$\dfrac{n^2 - n}{2} = \textit{no. of handshakes}$$

$$\dfrac{n - 1 \times n}{2} = \textit{no. of handshakes}$$

Although the solutions are clear the processes by which they reached them are not.

Some children went half way to discovering the rule and made the rest fit. Lindsey's group did just that (see Figure D).

Ruth, age 9, solved the problem quite easily at school. Then, during the half-term holiday, she watched a maths programme on television. She told me the programme was exploring the differences between some number patterns. This inspired her to find another way of solving the problem. She developed a complicated algorithm which works in the case of eight children shaking hands. She did not explore it any further than that until I talked to her about it. We have included it in this section because intrigued by her perseverance and confidence.

Knowing Why the Rule Works

ESTABLISHING A PROOF   Some of the older children were not content to find a rule. Encouraged by the teacher they went on to prove why the rule works.

Levels of Knowing

The sense of achievement felt by the children was very real. The confidence they gained from knowing they had 'cracked' the first part of the

The Rule

We knew that if everybody shaked hands with the rest and theirself the answer would be 49 or 7^2; but you can only shake hands with the other six so each person who didn't shake hand with theirself came to 7. This means $7^2 - 7 = 42$ this, however was not the answer because we had already found out that the answer was 21. Therefore we divided by 2. The rule $= (n^2 - n) \div 2$ or in this case $(7^2 - 7) \div 2$. We needed to work out a formula because we need to find out the answer for large numbers in a short period of time and as the A-B, A-C formula would not be appropriate.

FIG. D   *Making the rest fit the rule.*

problem gave them the incentive to continue. There seemed to be surges of energy and excitement followed by lulls and some frustration. These aspects of problem solving and investigational work are often overlooked. The relief and excitement of knowing are not seen very often in the classroom because teachers tend not to put themselves or the children at risk.

References

Billington, J. & P. Evans. 1986. "Levels of knowing." *Mathematics Teaching* 114:40–41.

Emerging goals in mathematics emphasize mathematics as communication in elementary school classrooms, but how to integrate writing and mathematics is not always clear. Joan Countryman describes the kinds of writing she does with her students, and the role it plays in developing their understanding. She connects her students' writing to the kind of mathematical communication encouraged in the Curriculum and Evaluation Standards *(NCTM 1989).*

Most striking for some readers is the notion that a research mathematician ought to have excellent communication skills. Why do you think this could be true? If you can, interview mathematicians in your community or at your local university. Do they agree that communication is essential?

As you read, reflect on your own experiences as a learner of mathematics. How has writing played a role in your mathematical learning?

Writing to Learn*

Joan Countryman

Parables

A standard parable is $y = x^2$ which looks like this Ψ. It keeps getting wider the farther you go up. All parables are symmetrical and have vertexes. If you add a number like $y = x^2 + 3$ the parable will move up on the graph. The opposite happens when you subtract a number. To make the graph skinnier multiply by a positive number, $10x^2$ or to make the parable wider multiply by a fraction $\frac{1}{4}x^2$. If you want to move a graph sideways try $y = x^2 - 2x$. That will move the graph to the left and down one. If $y = x^2 \div 2x$ the graph will move to the right and down one. If $y = -x^2$ the graph will turn upside down like this Λ. Parables are interesting figures.

—A seventh grader

Unless I am badly mistaken, the writing above is not about parables. Nor is it about teaching the difference between parables and parabolas (although this seventh grader could profit from such a lesson). This writing sample demonstrates the connections between writing and thinking and learning mathematics, which also happens to be the subject of this book.

For years, I have asked my students (in grades seven through

* Originally published in *Writing to Learn Mathematics: Strategies that Work*. Heinemann: Portsmouth, NH. 1992.

twelve) to write, read, and talk about what they are learning in math class. I want them to make sense of arithmetic, algebra, geometry, and calculus by putting into their own words the ideas and methods they are exploring. In little essays, like the one on parabolas, they record what they find. The rules and procedures of school mathematics make little sense to many students. They memorize examples, they follow instructions, they do their homework, and they take tests, but they cannot say what their answers mean. Even the successful ones claim, "I can do it, but I can't explain it." A student who says "page 73" when asked to describe what she is doing in algebra class is telling the truth: she is proceeding through the text, but she is not constructing for herself the mathematics she is trying to learn.

Knowing mathematics is doing mathematics. We need to create situations where students can be active, creative, and responsive to the physical world. I believe that to learn mathematics students must construct it for themselves. They can only do that by exploring, justifying, representing, discussing, using, describing, investigating, predicting, in short by being active in the world. Writing is an ideal activity for such processes.

A student complains, "Why do we have to write? This isn't English class; this is math." Many teachers and students resist the idea that writing belongs in math classrooms. Indeed some math teachers, like their strongest students, preferred mathematics because they imagined that it did not require much writing. Once in the classroom, however, these teachers soon realized that the practice of teaching requires making lists, notes, outlines, and plans, writing reports and comments. In addition, many math teachers agree that the way we really learn content—the arithmetic, algebra, geometry, and calculus that we teach—is by preparing lessons. Then we record our own struggle to explain the material to our students.

When students challenge me to show what writing has to do with math, I reply, "This *is* math. You know, it's fine to get the right answer, but what good is that answer if you can't explain it to anyone?" I tell them that the mathematician Henry Pollak lists the ability to communicate with others as one of the requirements for a good research mathematician. The productive use of language is a skill that all students should practice in all disciplines; reading, writing, and speaking belong in every classroom, even math classrooms.

Hence, over the years my students have recorded their work. They write about finding the slope of a line, about using the Pythagorean theorem; they describe how many squares there are on a checkerboard, how many handshakes are possible among a group of twenty people; they explain derivatives and integrals and fractions and integers.

My students write in a variety of genres. They write in journals:

> Math has gotten totally confusing. I have hated trig functions and logs and stuff from day one—and now to combine them with calculus. It's too much! I don't think calculus is my thing. I can't figure out if I'm really confused and incapable of understanding or just lazy (but then laziness would keep me from understanding so it would be both).

They freewrite:

> Algebra is math with a bunch of letters that stand for numbers. They are mystery letters. When you finish the problem the letters usually turn to numbers.
>
> —James

> Algebra is a form of math involving variables. You learn it in 8th grade.
>
> —Mike

> I think algebra is very hard and confusing. It builds on itself. What may seem easy grows till it becomes very hard.
>
> —Lisa

They write in learning logs:

Positives and Negatives

> In class we have been using $+$ and $-$. They are very hard to understand (especially subtraction of $+$ and $-$). When you are adding the same signs together $+6 + +8 = +14$ it is easy, you just do normal adding keeping the signs the same. If, however, the signs are different, $-4 + +6 + +2$, you just subtract and the higher numbers sign dominates. I'm very clear on adding. On subtracting I'm not so good although I am clear on how to do it. When you are subtracting two of the same signs $+10 - +6 = +4$ all you do is subtract. When the signs are different $-6 - +2$

-8 it is just adding and the higher number's sign dominates. But a hard one to solve is when the signs are different and the first digit is less than the second $(+4 - -7 = +11)$ the first digit's sign will be the sign in the answer then you just add. When the digits are the same signs but the number in front is smaller $(-3 - -7 = +4)$ you just subtract but you take the sign that is opposite from the problem's signs—for example if the problem's signs are $-$ the answer sign will be $+$. I don't understand why but I know how to do it.

—Gary

They write math autobiographies:

To begin with, I love math! I have always loved math, since 1st grade, and I will keep on loving math until I die. It started in first grade when I got my first arithmetic book. I worked very hard that year and by the end of the year I knew my times tables. In second grade I learned short division on my own in my spare time, while in school I started mental math. I was good at that. By the time third grade started, I was well into division and I could do a little bit of long division, too, which I perfected as the year went by. The next two years I learned things like decimals, percents etc. which I had already done in fourth grade. At the end of sixth grade my parents and I made a big decision: I went 7–2 and did seventh and eighth grade in one year. The math program in 7–2 was excellent! I did Algebra I during that year and I loved it.

I'm afraid of math. I always have been. Anytime anybody works on math with me, whether it is a friend, student, teacher, or family member, I freeze up. It's like all the math I have ever learned in my whole life has left my stream of consciousness. It's only after a long time of going over a problem that I can do it confidently and easily. I have been told my instincts are good, however, I'm always afraid to go with my first answer cause I think it will be wrong. I remember one time in 10th grade, the teacher asked the class to find an easy, logical way to go about doing this problem. Nobody could seem to find a good way. After about 10 minutes I volunteered my solution and he liked it. In fact, the whole class thought it was a good method. I felt very proud.

They write about math problems:

Our problem was to find a number with 13 factors. This is how our math class went about it:

To find this number our highly intelligible minds* knew a few things if we were to find this number. First, the number had to be a perfect square, the number would also have an odd number of factors. Second, the number's square had to be prime. Before we figured these clues out, we were randomly picking numbers from the top of our heads.

We looked at many numbers before we realized that if we doubled numbers (starting with the number one) it formed a steady pattern counting by ones. We kept doubling numbers and finding the number of factors until we reached the number that had 13 factors, which is. . . . .

4096!!!

*Just joking!

—Jenny

They write formal papers:

There are many stereotypes about mathematics: children do not like it, boys are better at it and so on. Many of these stereotypes do not hold true in the classroom. The goal of this project was to see if there is a correlation between age or sex or the child's attitude toward math and how well first grade students were able to transfer mathematical knowledge of three digit addition and subtraction of money.

A group of twenty-two first grade students were given a questionnaire which provided the data of this project. The questionnaire asked if the children liked math, if they found math hard or easy. The students had completed surveys like this one in the past and were accustomed to the format. They were also uninhibited to tell their true feelings. The survey then had ten problems of addition and subtraction of money (dollars and cents). The children have been doing three digit addition and subtraction for months using only numbers without the dollar signs and the decimal point. Their teacher expressed her confidence that all of the children could score 90% or higher on a simple test of addition or subtraction problems. When the signs were added, however, only twelve children were able to score a 90% or higher.

They even write test questions:

Graph f° g when $f(x) = |x|$ *and* $g(x) = x^2 - 4.$

Write a brief essay on how the graph of f°g *is different from the graph of* $x^2 - 4.$ *How do the domain and range differ?*

In whatever genre, writing can motivate and enhance the learning that takes place when students confront the concepts and procedures of mathematics. Listen to the voice of the eleventh grader who wrote this:

> I'm beginning to feel very comfortable on the computer. Before, I had the ability to plot a graph, but now I can manipulate the different points and view them as an index, a sort of enlarged table of values. Working with that I can find zeros, turning points, etc. I wonder how to do the slopes of curves. The difference between two points changes when looking at different parts of the curve. I wonder if it is in some way related to the differences between arithmetic and squared series.
>
> $$\begin{array}{cccccc} 1 & 3 & 5 & 7 & 9 & 11 \\ & 2 & 2 & 2 & 2 & 2 \end{array}$$
>
> $$\begin{array}{cccccc} 1 & 4 & 9 & 16 & 25 & 36 \\ & 3 & 5 & 7 & 9 & 11 \\ & & 2 & 2 & 2 & 2 \end{array}$$
>
> The differences (changes in Y) must have something to do with the slope of a parabola.

Listen again:

- Writing helps students become aware of what they know and do not know, can and cannot do: "I'm beginning to feel comfortable on the computer. . . ."
- When students write they connect their prior knowledge with what they are studying: "Before I had the ability to plot a graph, but now I can manipulate. . . ."
- They summarize their knowledge and give teachers insights into their understanding: ". . . I can find zeros, turning points, etc."
- They raise questions about new ideas: "I wonder how to do the slopes of curves."
- They reflect on what they know: "The difference between two points changes. . . ."
- They construct mathematics for themselves: "The differences must have something to do with the slope. . . ."

When students use language to find out what they think about mathematics, the result is often surprising. "The very fact that [the teacher] assigned writing was enough to make me start thinking," one student said of his calculus class. "We all thought this writing was ridiculous at first, but I've come to see it as the most important thing we did all year."

The connection between writing and mathematics became obvious and important to this student because of *the writing and the mathematics* that he did that year. Had he been taught mathematics as it has traditionally been taught, writing would not have made much sense. The use of writing in mathematics class, as described in this book, presupposes a different view of mathematics and mathematics instruction. In this view, mathematics is a way of thinking about the world. To understand what mathematics is we need to look at what mathematicians do, for this is a human endeavor, a thinking process the results of which come from the work of human minds.

Unfortunately, school mathematics gives our students the impression that mathematics is a dead subject, that all of its truths were discovered before 1700, when indeed considerably more mathematics has been developed and published since 1945 than in all the years of human history before that time. Little of that knowledge appears in the elementary and secondary curriculums, both of which continue to emphasize paper and pencil manipulation of symbols. An eighth grader who wrote that "Math to me shouldn't have to be anything more than $+, -, \times, \div$" was speaking for a large percentage of students whose vision of the discipline has been shaped by an arithmetic-driven elementary school curriculum.

Mathematicians have described a shift in contemporary mathematics away from emphasis on number and space and toward pattern and application. The distinction between pure mathematics and applied mathematics is blurring, happily, and some of the methods that have emerged—mathematical modeling, graph theory, and data analysis, for example—are accessible to younger students. These methods provide opportunities even for students in elementary grades to do real mathematics. As the following journal entry suggests, students find the work with real data compelling:

> The problems in section 21 are enticing, they seem so real. World population, half-lives of radioactive isotopes, all these things are

so physical. The ability to develop mathematical models for all this stuff is refreshing. No more of that—but what does this have to do with real life?—stuff.

The intelligent citizen of the twenty-first century needs to know how to analyze data, how to reason in probabilistic situations, and how to make choices. What do the statistics about air quality on the front page of my newspaper mean? How should I think about situations that have a low probability of occurring but engender high risk? For example, what does a probability of one in a thousand mean in a discussion of radioactive emissions from a nuclear weapons plant? What questions should I pose to my senator about the data presented in a report on the depletion of the ozone layer?

Students at all levels need experience in identifying the kind of answer they want in a given situation. Should it be exact, or will an approximation do? Students need to know and to understand the advantages of different methods of obtaining answers. They need to know when to guess, when to use pencil and paper, when to use a calculator, how to recognize an answer, and whether the answer makes sense. A first grader, explaining how she used a calculator to find a sum, wrote:

> I added 28 + 10 − 5 and it turned out to be 33 when I pressed equals and I did the thinking.

The supermarket shopper uses estimation to be certain that the ten dollars he has in his wallet will cover the cost. At the cash register it matters whether the bill is $6.28 or $62.80. Technology, particularly calculators and computers, can allow teachers and students to function at a level higher than simple addition. While the machines perform mechanical operations the time saved can be spent inferring, organizing, interpreting, explaining, constructing, planning, and reflecting.

In 1989 the National Council of Teachers of Mathematics published *The Curriculum and Evaluation Standards for School Mathematics,* a report that reflects much of this new thinking about the need for change in the mathematics curriculum. Throughout the *Standards* three features of mathematics are emphasized:

1. Knowing mathematics is doing mathematics.
2. Technology has had enormous impact on the way that mathematics is done.

3. Mathematics is now in a "golden age of production" using new methods and addressing new questions.

Fifty-four standards covering grades K–12 present new methods and questions for teachers to use in the classroom. The standards on mathematics as communication reflect the view that "to know mathematics is to engage in a quest to understand and communicate."

The language of the *Standards* reflects that emphasis on understanding and communicating. Here are a few excerpts, first from the standards for grades K–4, which state that students should be able to "relate physical materials, pictures, and diagrams to mathematical ideas," "reflect on and clarify their thinking about mathematical ideas and situations," and "relate their everyday language to mathematical language and symbols."

In grades 5–8, students are expected to "reflect and clarify their own thinking about mathematical ideas and situations," "use the skills of reading, listening, and viewing to interpret and evaluate mathematical ideas," and "discuss mathematical ideas and make conjectures and convincing arguments."

In grades 9–12, students should learn to "reflect upon and clarify their thinking about mathematical ideas and relationships," "formulate mathematical definitions and express generalizations discovered through investigations," and "express mathematical ideas orally and in writing."

With such a clear emphasis on understanding and communicating, it shouldn't be surprising that math teachers have been turning to writing.

Most teachers know that successful learning requires reinforcement, feedback, synthesis, and action. Certain attributes of writing correspond with each of these. Writing strengthens a student's experience of a new concept. Students get immediate feedback from the words that they produce. When students write, they are integrating the work of the hand, the eye, and the brain. They fix on the page connections and relationships between what they already know and what they are meeting for the first time. When they write, students are active and engaged.

It is the activity that appeals to me. Writing gets everyone involved. In *Writing to Learn* (1988), William Zinsser examines the fear of writing and traces the potential of writing-across-the-curriculum. When Zinsser visited my eleventh-grade precalculus class he found students writing about trigonometry.

> Mrs. Countryman drew a triangle on the blackboard and told the class she wanted them to determine the size of its three angles. But she gave them none of the information they would need—for instance, the length of the sides.
>
> "I want you to write how you might go about solving this problem when you do get more information from me," she said. The students wrote for about five minutes. They looked like writers—they were thinking hard and laboriously putting sentences on paper and crossing out sentences that obviously didn't express what they were thinking, perhaps because their thinking kept changing as they wrote and discovered what they really thought. They even sounded like writers; I heard the scratching out of words that is the obbligato of a writer's life.
>
> After that some of them were asked to read what they had written. The papers were all brief journeys into logic: if I knew *this* I'd be able to find out *that*; what I need to determine is *a*, so the best method to use is probably *x* and *y*. Writing and thinking and learning had merged into one process. (165–66)

The Writing Process

Writing, of course, takes many forms. Proponents of process writing describe three broad categories of student work: expository, expressive, and personal writing. Expository writing, which has structure and rules, is most common in schools. Expressive writing often takes the form of stories or poems. There is evidence that the best expository and expressive work evolves from personal writing, which is closest to inner speech and to the thinking process. This is the writing that helps us come to terms with new ideas. It takes the form of notes, letters, or journal entries, and is not governed by rules of grammar or syntax. When students learn to use language to find out what they think they become better writers and thinkers. Our students need more classroom opportunities to do informal writing, to make sense by making meaning, to create for themselves the underlying concepts of mathematics.

Writing mathematics can free students of the assumption that math is just a collection of right answers to questions posed by someone else. Writing—and this includes writing notes, lists, observations, feelings, in addition to term papers, lab reports, and essay questions—will expand the narrow view of mathematics that many students carry around in their heads, a view reflected in this journal entry:

> Math to me shouldn't have to be anything more than $+$, $-$, $\times$, $\div$. All of the other math is really ridiculous to have. I think that if you would like to know how to do all that math you should be able to learn, but if you don't want to you shouldn't.
>
> —Kate (an eighth grader)

Our goals—in math and in all disciplines—are much more ambitious than Kate's. We want students to learn to interpret unfamiliar texts, to construct convincing arguments, to understand complex systems, to develop new approaches to problems, and to negotiate the resolution of those problems in groups, to pose questions and to evaluate alternative responses to those questions. The skills they need to reach those goals are also the same. Students need opportunities to organize, interpret, and explain, to construct, symbolize, and communicate, to plan, infer, and reflect. Practicing these fundamental skills will help them learn mathematics.

References

National Council of Teachers of Mathematics. 1989. *Curriculum and Evaluation Standards for School Mathematics, K–12*. Reston, VA: National Council of Teachers of Mathematics.

Zinsser, W. 1988. *Writing to Learn*. New York: HarperCollins.

"Every time we push an idea to its limits, we find out how it relates to areas that might have seemed to have nothing to do with it. By virtue of that search, our understanding of the world is deepened and broadened."

Complex ideas develop over time and are not nurtured by the impulse for tidiness and closure that often characterizes school learning. For both adults and children, Eleanor Duckworth advocates leaving "time for confusion." Her detailed examples taken from teacher study groups are compelling illustrations of the kind of learning she describes.

Many teachers recognize both the importance of learning over an extended period and the tension that comes from fitting this to the demands of a school schedule. Confusion, cognitive dissonance, and the role of misunderstanding in learning are some of Duckworth's themes.

Learning in Breadth and Depth*

Eleanor Duckworth

If ideas develop on their own so slowly, what can we do to speed them up? In Chapter 3, we pointed out that Piaget referred to this as "the American question." For him the question is not how *fast* you go but how *far* you go. He delighted in the results of a study of kittens carried out by Howard Gruber. Studying his own children, Piaget had concluded that they were about a year old before they realized that an object had its own continuing existence and location even when out of their reach and out of their sight. Gruber found that kittens go through all the same steps that children do, but instead of taking a year, they take six weeks (Gruber et al., 1971). Piaget cheerfully pointed out that you can scarcely say that kittens are better off for having cut almost a year off the time. After all, they don't get much further.

How could it be that going fast does not mean going far? A useful metaphor might be the construction of a tower—all the more appropriate given that Piaget thinks of the development of intelligence as continual construction. Building a tower with one brick on top of another is a pretty speedy business. But the tower will soon reach its limits, compared with one built on a broad base or a deep foundation— which of course takes a longer time to construct.

What is the intellectual equivalent of building in breadth and depth? I think it is a matter of making connections: Breadth could be thought of as the widely different spheres of experience that can be related to one another; depth could be thought of as the many different

* Originally published in *The Having of Wonderful Ideas*, pp. 70–82. New York: Teachers College Press. 1987.

kinds of connections that can be made among different facets of our experience. I am not sure whether intellectual breadth and depth can be separated from each other, except in talking about them. In this chapter I shall not try to keep them separate, but instead try to show how learning with breadth and depth is a different matter from learning with speed.

Productive Wrong Ideas

If a child spends time exploring all the possibilities of a given notion, it may mean that she holds onto it longer, and moves onto the next stage less quickly; but by the time she does move on, she will have a far better foundation—the idea will serve her far better, will stand up in the face of surprises. Let me develop a hypothetical example to show what I mean, based on the notion of the conservation of area.

Imagine two identical pieces of paper; you cut one in half and rearrange the pieces so the shape is different from the original one, while preserving the same area, as in the example in Figure A. One might think that it would be to anyone's advantage to realize early in life that a change in shape does not affect area; that no matter how a shape is transformed, its area is conserved. But I can imagine a child not managing to settle that question as soon as others because she raises for herself the question of the perimeter. In fact the perimeter *does* change, and thinking about the relationship between those two is complicated work. One child might, then, take longer than another to come to the conclusion that area is conserved, independent of shape, but her understanding will be the better for it. Most children (and adults) who arrive smartly at the notion that area is independent of shape do not think about the perimeter and are likely to become confounded if it is brought up. Having thought about perimeter on her own, she has complicated the job of thinking about area, but once she has straightened it out, her understanding is far deeper than that of someone who has never noticed this difference between area and perimeter.

Exploring ideas can only be to the good, even if it takes time. Wrong ideas, moreover, can only be productive. Any wrong idea that is corrected provides far more depth than if one never had a wrong idea to begin with. You master the idea much more thoroughly if you have

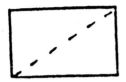 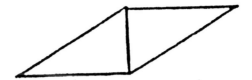

FIG. A

explored alternatives, tried to work it out in areas where it didn't work, and figured out why it was that it didn't work, all of which takes time.

After this hypothetical introduction, here are some examples where making the mistakes and correcting them reveal and give rise to a far better grasp of the phenomenon than there would have been if no mistakes were made at all.

One experiment involves an odd-shaped lake like the one in Figure B with a road around it, and a bi-colored car on the road, one side black and one side white. Let's say the white side is next to the water to start with; the question is, after the car drives around a corner, or around several corners, which color will be beside the water? Six-year-olds, after one or two mistaken predictions, usually come to be quite sure that it will always be the white. Eight-year-olds, on the other hand, can be very perplexed, and not quite get it straight, no matter how often they see the white side come out next to the water. They keep predicting that *this* time the black side will be next to the water.

Now one might be tempted to think that 6-year-olds know more than 8-year-olds. They, after all, do not make mistakes. But I think it is the greater breadth and depth of the 8-year-olds' insight that leads to their perplexity. Eight-year-olds are often just at the point of organizing space into some interrelated whole: Your left is opposite my right; something that you can see from your point of view may be hidden from my point of view; if a car in front of me is facing right, I see its right side, and if it turns 180°, I'll see its left side. With all these shifting, relative relationships, what is it about the lake that makes *that* relationship an absolute? No matter how many curves there are in the road, the same side is always next to the water. If a car turns 180°, I

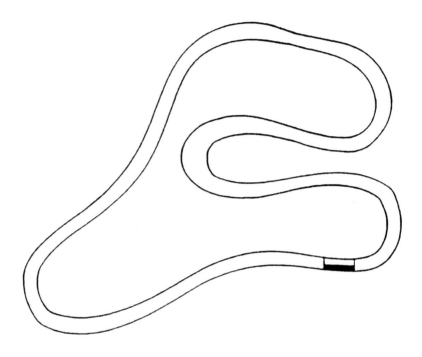

FIG. B

thought I would see its other side; well, how is it that the *same* side
is next to the water? What is it that stays the same and what is it that
changes, after all? The 6-year-old, who has no idea of the systematic
changes involved in some spatial relationships, has no difficulty seeing
the constant in the lake problem; it is because the 8-year-old is trying
to make sense of the lake in a far broader context that the right answer
is not so immediate. The dawning organization of something new throws
into confusion something that had been simple before. But when, a few
months later, the 8- or 9-year-old does start to understand that the
same side must always stay next to the lake, his or her understanding
is far deeper than that of the 6-year-old; it is set in the context of an
understanding of spatial relationships as a whole.

Here is another example, where what appears to be less facility
really indicates greater understanding. I was working with two children,
who happened to be brother and sister, and they were making all possible

```
R  B  Y              G  R  B  Y

R  Y  B              R  G  Y  B

B  R  Y              B  R  G  Y

B  Y  R              B  Y  R  G

Y  R  B

Y  B  R
```

FIG. C

arrangements of three colors. After each of them had found all six possibilities, I added a fourth color, and they tried again. The sister, who was younger, rapidly produced a dozen, and was still going. The older brother stopped at four, and declared that that's all there were. But look at what he had done. With three colors, he had made the arrangement shown in Figure C (left). Now, into what he had already, he inserted the fourth color, in each of the possible positions as shown in Figure C (right). It was *because* of his sense of system—his sense (which can only be called mathematical) that there was a fixed and necessary number of placements—that he stopped there: The new color was in each possible position, within a system that had all of the other colors already in each possible position. It is true that his thinking left out one step, but nonetheless his was a far deeper understanding of permutations than his sister's facile but random generation of yet more arrangements that looked different.

Ways of Measuring—Productive and Unproductive

Getting closer to everyday concerns in the classroom, think of measurement. It can seem very straightforward—count the number of units that apply to some quantity and there it is, measured: so many foot-long rulers in a table, plus a number of inches; so many minutes in the running of a mile, plus a number of seconds. But take this example, for which I am indebted to Strauss, Stavy, and Orpag (1981): You've measured the temperature of one glass of water—100°; you add to it another glass of water, which is also 100°. What will the temperature be now? Most of our measurement experience would lead us to say 200°! And that is what a lot of children do in fact say—having easily understood *how* to add measurements together, but never having wondered *when* or *whether* to add measurements together.

Let me, by contrast, give some examples of invention of ways of measuring, which might seem tedious and inefficient, but which are thoroughly understood by their inventors. The first one deserves a better accounting than I can undertake here. In a class studying (once again) pendulums, children had explored coupled pendulums, set up like the example in Figure D. If everything is symmetrical when you start one bob, then after a few swings the other bob starts to move, gradually bob *A*'s movement diminishes and bob *B*'s movement increases, until *A* is stopped and *B* is swinging widely. Then the movement passes back to *A*, and so on. Suppose, however, that everything is not symmetrical— the stick is tilted, or one string is longer than the other, or one bob weighs more than the other. In that case, the bob that starts swinging does pass some of its movement on to the other, but it does not come to a halt itself; the halts are asymmetric—they belong only to the bob that was at rest when the other started swinging.

That is a long introduction. The point is that in this class, a time came when the children were interested in comparing the weights of the wooden bobs and the steel bobs. Scales were available, and most of the children went to them. But Elliott, who happened to be the least scholarly child in the class, had a different idea. He set up a coupled pendulum, hung a steel bob on one string, and then added wooden bobs to the other, trying the coupled motion each time he added a bob—until, at four wooden bobs, the halts were alternating symmetrically from string to string. So he knew the four on one string must weigh the same as the one on the other. This astonishingly imaginative grasp of what it means to compare weights of things should be contrasted with the following tale.

In a different pendulum class, junior high school students had

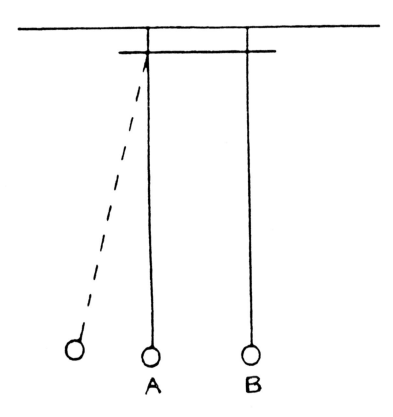

FIG. D

just previously been taught the equilibrium formula that applies to balances: Distance times weight on one side must equal distance times weight on the other. The only weighing mechanism available to them now was a strip of pegboard, supported in the center (Figure E). When the students became interested in weighing the bobs, they hung a wooden bob on one end, and then a steel bob on the other side, so as to make the pegboard horizontal, announcing, "There, they weigh the same. We learned that just last week, they weigh the same." It seemed clear that that formula had been hastily learned, and remained quite unexplored.

The next example comes from work done with Jeanne Bamberger

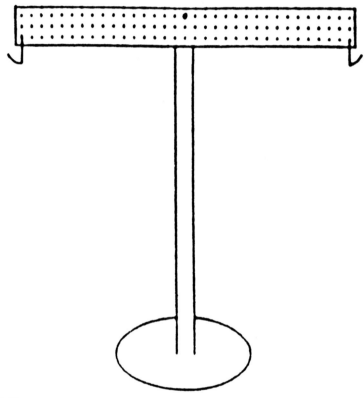

FIG. E

and Magdalene Lampert at the Massachusetts Institute of Technology. We were working with a group of Cambridge teachers, helping them examine their own ways of knowing in order to better understand children's ways of knowing. One kind of knowledge we were exploring was music. They were building tunes, and at one point they wanted to know whether a tune they had built had sections that were the same length. They didn't know how to think about that. They tried to use a watch but couldn't tell from a watch whether the first half of the tune was the same length as the second half. This led us to invent time-measuring machines. We took a recorded tune, as the standard event, and they were to construct time machines (without using watches or clocks) to tell whether some other piece of music, which we were subsequently going to play, was as long as that first piece, or longer, or shorter. They all made what we called tune-specific time-measuring machines; that is, they did not set out to find some unit that would be repeated a number of times, but instead tried to make something that measured just the length of the standard piece: water dripping out of a cup, down to a line that indicated the end of the piece; or a candle burning down just to the end of the piece.

One team made a ramp of two pieces of metal, each about 4 feet long. To their dismay, the ball rolled off the 8 feet of ramp before the music stopped. They changed the slope; the ball still rolled off. They made a pathway on the floor at the end out of tongue depressors so that the ball could keep rolling along the floor, but now the ball stopped too soon. They changed the slope—very steep, barely any slope at all—but no matter what they did with the slope, the ball stopped too soon. They finally concluded that they would have to make the ball do something else after the roll down the ramp; otherwise they would simply have to abandon the ramp idea. So they moved the ramp up onto a long table, set it up with barely any slope at all, and arranged it so the ball could drop off at the end. Now what could they have it do when it dropped off? Casting about for available material, they took a pan from one of the pan balances, and suspended it at the end of the ramp, so the ball would fall into it (Figure F). As the recorded tune started, the ball started rolling slowly down the ramp, fell into the pan at the end, thus setting it swinging, and at 32 swings of the pan the tune was ended. A single-purpose time machine it was, but a perfectly dependable one—it was a roll down the ramp followed by 32 swings of the pan, every time. The tune that was to be compared with it, moreover, turned out to be a roll down the ramp followed by 37 swings of the pan; so their machine was shown to be adequate to its time-measuring task.

These stories can be thought of as comic relief. In a sense, they are. But the comedy of the coupled pendulum and the ball on the ramp is very different from the comedy of the 200° water and the misuse of the pegboard balance. The latter two are sad tales of too rapid assumption of understanding. The other two are the rather appealing consequences of avoiding such facile rapidity. How to measure can be taught rapidly, but when it is, the inadequacies are stunning.

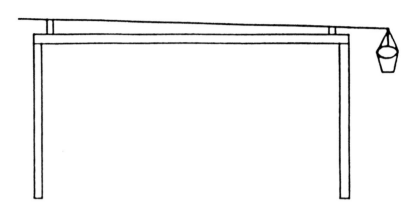

FIG. F

It is quite different from the breadth and depth of understanding involved in messily constructing your own ways of measuring, knowing what they mean, how they are applicable or not applicable, and how they inform each new situation.

Raising Questions About Simple Answers

Readers may think that any adult must of course know what time measurement is about, and that the only challenge in the work of these teachers was the technological one of getting some machine to work dependably. But it is worth reflecting on how you would know, without having some other ready-made timer, whether a candle burns with the same speed during its first quarter-inch and during its last quarter-inch. How do we know that a sweep second hand takes the same time for each one of its sweeps? How, back there in history, did anyone conclude that some event always takes the same amount of time, and so could be used to measure the time of other events? Without a standard unit, how did they establish a standard unit? This group of teachers gave those questions a lot of thought. And here is a question that gave them pause for a long time: One of them had heard that between five and seven in the evening, demands on electricity are such that electric clocks always run slower. Is that true? If it were, how would we ever know? If it is not, why isn't it? Wouldn't any time piece, in fact, keep going slower and slower as the battery wears out, or as the spring unwinds? As teachers, I think one major role is to *undo* rapid assumptions of understanding, to slow down closure, in the interests of breadth and depth, which attach our knowledge to the world in which we are called upon to use it. There may, for some given situation, be one right answer, even one that is quite easily reached. But I think a teacher's job is to raise questions about even such a simple right answer, to push it to its limits, to see where it holds up and where it does not hold up. One right answer unconnected to other answers, unexplored, not pushed to its limits, necessarily means a less adequate grasp of our experience. Every time we push an idea to its limits, we find out how it relates to areas that might have seemed to have nothing to do with it. By virtue of that search, our understanding of the world is deepened and broadened.

I would like to develop this thought in the context of the adult thinking of this same group of teachers. Having started with music and proceeding to measure time, they came to the study of ramps, and the main interest of this study was that they pushed the limits of what seemed to be ordinary, even obvious, thoughts about time, speed, and space.

The tune-specific time-measurement machines developed in the direction of a search for units of time measurement—calibrating the candle as it burned, counting the water drips, looking for natural phenomena that keep a steady rhythm. The search applied to ramps, too: Could a ball rolling down a ramp give rise to units of time? This led to another question, as a preliminary: What does the speed of a ball do as it rolls down a ramp? Does it remain constant? Increase? Decrease and then increase? Increase and then remain constant?

One group, watching a ball in order to make an initial guess about the answer, noticed a spot on it. The spot came up faster and faster as the ball rolled, until by the last part of the ramp its occurrences were no longer distinguishable—it looked like a blurred continuous line. This supported the idea that the ball was going faster and faster as it rolled down the ramp, but this group wanted to do a better job of it than that. It occurred to one of them that if the dot left a mark as it rolled they would be able to see better what the speed of the ball was doing. A bit of experimenting and they found a substance they could mark the dot with that would leave a spot each time it hit a long sheet of computer printout paper that was stretched down the ramp. The reader might want to predict what the spots did. We have since discovered that about half the adults we ask predict that the dots will get closer together, a few predict they will get farther apart, and the rest predict they will remain at a constant distance. The roll of computer paper with the spots left by the ball looked like the top graph in Figure G. The reaction of at least one member of the group was to take a piece of string and measure the distances, saying something to the effect of, "Gee, those dots don't get closer together as noticeably as I had thought they would!"

That turned out to be just the beginning of many perplexities in this consideration of speed-space-time relationships. Another group, also trying to establish what the speed of a ball does as the ball rolls down a ramp, produced the bottom graph shown in Figure G. At a subsequent seminar, the teachers who had been absent when the two graphs were produced were given the job of interpreting them—trying to establish how each had been made, and what each of them said about the speed of the balls rolling down the ramps.

I am not going to say here how the second graph came about. My purposes are better served if readers put themselves to the task—because in this case the answer to the ball-ramp problem is really beside the point; what I would rather do is make vivid how much harder it is to think coherently about space-speed-time phenomena than it is to enunciate formulas.

Here are a couple of the inferences made by the members of the original group. One person thought the spots on the first graph looked as if the ball had left its own mark as it rolled; but then, she went on to say, it would have to have been rolling at the same speed all the way, so it couldn't have been rolling down a ramp. The second graph was thought *not* to have been made by the ball itself. This inference was made not on the basis of the distances between the marks, but because the marks looked as if they were drawn by a hand-held felt marker. One generally accepted thought was that marks were made indicating where the ball was after equal time intervals.

The discussion of these two graphs went on for two hours. The members of the group who had been present to generate them got caught up in considering what interpretations were possible in addition to those they knew to be the case. Does the first graph say anything about speed? Is anything to be learned by superimposing the

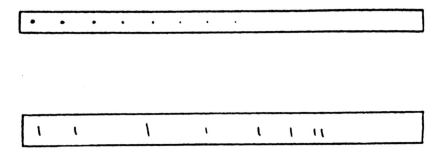

FIG. G

first graph on the second? What picture would you get if you made both graphs at once, of one ball rolling down a ramp? What *does* the speed of the ball do in the second graph, anyway? The point of this work was to build a construction of space-time-speed ideas not rapidly, but solidly, and to know what the relationships are, after all, that are summed up in that easy high school formula. At the end of those two hours (which, remember, followed a number of other hours of experimental work and thought), no matter how I pushed the conclusions into paradoxical or counter-intuitional extremes, the teachers resisted. No one could be seduced by what sounded like a sensible thought if it did not fit into the idea-structure that they had created, in all of its breadth and depth.

Time for Confusion

One other topic that this group of teachers worked on was the moon. All of us know that the earth turns upon itself, the moon goes around the earth, and while both these things are going on, the earth is also going around the sun. All of us also see the sky get light and dark again every day, see the sun pass overhead, often see the moon, sometimes full and sometimes not. But how many of us can make a connection between these two kinds of experience? On a given afternoon in Massachusetts, for example, at 5:00, the moon was slightly less than half, and it was visible quite high in the sky. Now, in a model of sun, earth, and moon, could you place them in the relative positions to indicate where they would be in order for the sky to look like that? Almost nobody I've run into can do that. Those two kinds of knowledge about the moon are, for the most part, quite separate. Bringing them together, moreover, is a difficult job, which makes this a marvelous subject through which to study one's ways of making sense of one's experience, and especially to realize how a simple formal model can have almost no connection with the experience it is meant to describe.

It takes months of watching and finding some order in the motions before one can know, when looking at the moon, in what direction it will move from there; where it will be an hour later, or 24 hours later; how the crescent will be tipped 2 hours from now; whether it has yet reached its highest point of the night; whether, tomorrow, it will be visible in the daytime. Does the moon pass every day straight overhead? Does the moon ever pass straight overhead? Does it depend on where you are on the earth? If, right now, from here, it was up at a 70° angle from me, at what angle would it be if I climbed up to the top of that building? If I were sitting down, at what angle would it be? Or if I walked down the block toward it?

One friend claimed he had seen the moon like the drawing in Figure H (left). How was it possible, he asked, for the round earth to have cast a crescent-shaped shadow on the moon? He could understand seeing the moon itself like a crescent, as in Figure H (right), but he could not understand what he claimed to have seen. It is a good question for moon-watchers, and I put it to the readers, with what seem to me three possible explanations: Either he did not see the moon shaped that way; or there are circumstances under which a sphere (the earth, in this case) can cast a crescent-shaped shadow; or the crescent that is missing from the side of the moon is not the shadow of the earth.

Another friend confessed how perplexed she had been when she realized that people standing on the moon looked *up* to see the earth. Surely, from the moon, one should look down at the earth if, from the earth, one looks up at the moon? Figuring out that puzzle for herself was a source of considerable joy.

In our seminar, moon questions took us into sun-earth questions that were no less difficult. How, with models of earth and sun, do you

FIG. H

represent the sun coming up over the horizon? What is the horizon, anyway? If the sun is, for you, on the horizon, where is it for everybody else? If the sun is straight overhead at noon (and *is* it straight overhead at noon?), is it straight underfoot at midnight? If the sun's rays go out in all directions, past the earth, can we see them? Does that mean that the part that is in darkness on earth is smaller than the part that is in light?

One of the teachers drew on the blackboard this picture of the earth in the midst of the sun's rays (Figure I), and was trying to articulate her thoughts about it. Another member of the group was asking her to be more precise. Did she mean *exactly* half the earth was in darkness? Did it get suddenly black at the dividing line, or was there some gray stripe? The one who was trying to articulate her thoughts grew angry, and gave up the attempt. She said later that she knew the questions were necessary at some point, but she had not been ready to be more precise. She was struggling to make sense of a morass of observations and models, an idea was just starting to take shape, and, she said, "I needed time for my confusion."

That phrase has become a touchstone for me. There is, of course, no particular reason to build broad and deep knowledge about ramps, pendulums, or the moon. I choose them, both in my teaching and in discussion here, to stand for any complex knowledge. Teachers are often, and understandably, impatient for their students to develop clear and adequate ideas. But putting ideas in relation to each other is not a simple job. It *is* confusing; and that confusion *does* take time. All of us need time for our confusion if we are to build the breadth and depth that give significance to our knowledge.

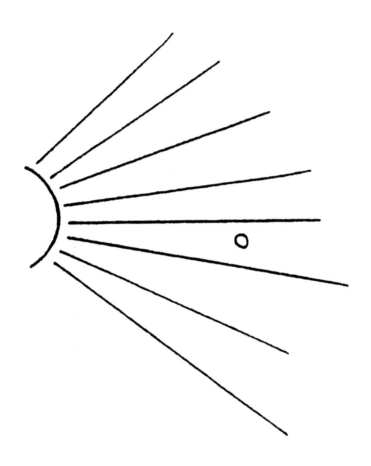

FIG. I

References

Gruber, H. E., J. S. Girgus & A. Banuazizi. 1971. "The Development of Object Permanence in Cats." *Developmental Psychology* (4):9–15.

Strauss, S., R. Stavy & N. Orpag. 1981. "The Child's Development of the Concept of Temperature." Cited in *Unshaped Behavioral Growth*, ed. S. Strauss with R. Levy. 1982. New York: Academic Press.

Combining references from Martin Buber, Shakespeare, Hindu philosophy, and physics with his personal experiences, David Hawkins describes learning relationships in terms of a triangle—the "I, Thou, and It." He believes mutual respect between adult and child is best developed when both parties focus on something other than themselves (i.e., the "it," or the "stuff" of learning). For Hawkins, finding an "it" that piques children's interests is the essential challenge in teaching.

Hawkins's article provides a way of seeing the importance of the search for the "right" activity or object to start a mathematical discussion and supports teachers in looking for a good starting point *rather than a perfect* lesson. One teacher found that this essay "dramatically increased my understanding and appreciation of the 'it.' . . . Even if the 'thou' disappears for a while I don't think I can ever return to that purely linear 'me–it' relationship with math again."

As you consider your own mathematics experiences, you might speculate on what makes an effective "it" for you and what it might be for your students.

I, Thou, and It*

David Hawkins

A proper and serious study of childhood would raise questions, I think, about one tendency widespread among us. Reference to it is there by implication in the previous essay with its suggestion that we send "emissaries to childhood." But of course that is only half the need; the other is to recognize that we will learn in the process only what we are prepared to observe and accept. Being repelled by the typical formality and sterility of our institutional treatment of children, many of us react by seeking and advocating patterns of association which are arranged for easy two-way communication, warm and loving. If that is half the story, it is a half which needs redefinition when the whole story is told. Long before Bettelheim, Immanuel Kant had given profound support to the proposition that, in human affairs generally, "love is not enough." The more basic gift is not love but respect, respect for others as ends in themselves, as actual and potential artisans of their own learnings and doings, of their own lives; and as thus uniquely contributing, in turn, to the learnings and doings of others.

Respect for the young is not a passive, hands-off attitude. It invites our own offering of resources, it moves us toward the furtherance of their lives and thus even, at times, toward remonstrance or intervention. Respect resembles love in its implicit aim of furtherance, but love without respect can blind and bind. Love is private and unbidden, whereas respect is implicit in all moral relations with others.

To have respect for children is more than recognizing their potentialities in the abstract, it is also to seek out and value their accomplishments—however small these may appear by the normal standards of

* Originally published in *The Informed Vision*, pp. 48–62. New York: Pantheon. 1980.

adults. But if we follow this track of thinking one thing stands out. We must provide for children those kinds of environments which elicit their interests and talents and which deepen their engagement in practice and thought. An environment of "loving" adults who are themselves alienated from the world around them is an educational vacuum. Adults involved in the world of man and nature bring that world with them to children, bounded and made safe to be sure, but not thereby losing its richness and promise of novelty. It was this emphasis which made me insist upon the third pronoun in the title, the impersonal "It" alongside the "I" and "Thou." Adults and children, like adults with each other, can associate well only in worthy interests and pursuits, only through a community of subject-matter and engagement which extends beyond the circle of their intimacy.

The attitude of deprecating subject-matter, and of deprecating curriculum as a guide to the providing of worthy subject-matter, reflects therefore the half-truth badly used.

Such is the background. As to the foreground of the following essay, some readers will astutely recognize in it a principled opposition to a widely popular belief in the efficacy of certain patented techniques of group association and therapy which are levered upon the art of inducing personal "confrontation," or some equivalent form of what I have called "artificial intimacy." Some of my friends disagree about Group Dynamics not so much in theory as in practice. They may agree that good human association must of course be premised upon common concerns and commitments with respect to what is "out there," something not "I" and not "Thou." But even without such commitment, they say, it works.

I think their attitude is rather like that expressed in a story about the physicist Niels Bohr. When a friend saw a horseshoe over the door of Bohr's country cabin, he said in mock astonishment, "Surely you don't believe in that old superstition!" "No," said Bohr, "but they say it works even if you don't believe in it."

I, Thou, and It

(1967)

I want to talk about children's understanding in the context of a proper education, more specifically of a good school. My topic, therefore, is the relationship between the teacher and the child and a third thing in the picture which has to be there and which completes the triangle of my title.

This is a relationship that has been much talked about, but truncated too often. People have made analogies between the teacher-child relationship and many other sorts of relationships. For example, in olden times people said, "What this child needs is good hard work and discipline," and that sounds rather like a parent-child relationship, doesn't it? Or they said, more recently, "The child needs love." That also sounds rather like a parent-child relationship. I'm sure that neither of these statements is completely false, but it seems to me they're both very unsatisfactory and that the relationship between the teacher and the child is something quite unique that isn't exactly paralleled by any other kind of human relationship. It's interesting to explore what is involved in it.

I know one rather good teacher who says he doesn't like children. He says this, I'm sure, with a rather special meaning of the word "like." He doesn't like children to be bewildered, at loose ends, not learning, and therefore he tries to get them over this as soon as possible. I mention him because I think the attitude of love, which is the parental attitude, isn't really the appropriate one. Perhaps the word "respect" might be more appropriate. I don't want to deny a very important element of affection for children in the make-up of good teachers, but the essence of the relationship is not that. It is a personal relationship, but it's not that kind of personal relationship. I want to talk about this in the context of the kind of thing we've been investigating in recent years, in the context of a kind of schooling we are interested in exploring further, marked by the more frequent and more abundant use of concrete materials by children in schools, *and* by their greater freedom of choice within this enriched world. I'd like to talk about how the third corner of the triangle affects the relations between the other two corners, how the "It" enters into the pattern of mutual interest and exchange between the teacher and the child. Being an incurable academic philosopher, I'd like to start on a very large scale and talk about human beings—of which children are presumably rather typical examples.

There's a tradition in philosophy which always comes to my mind when I'm thinking about this kind of question and which seems to be a more significant tradition than some others. It's a tradition which is expressed by saying, in one way or another, that people don't amount to very much except in terms of their involvement in what is outside and beyond them. A human being is a localized physical body, but you can't see him as a *person* unless you see him in his working relationships with the world around him. The more you cut off these working relationships, the more you put him in a box, figuratively or literally, the more you diminish him. Finally, when you've narrowed him down to nothing more than the surface of the skin and what's inside, without allowing him any kind of relationship with the world around him, you don't have very much left.

The ancient Hindu philosophers expressed this definition of human nature by using the metaphor of the mirror. In the *Baghavad Gita*, the Hindu scripture, there is a marvelous image of the soul which is said to be "the reflection of the rose in a glass." Like most religious philosophy, this one is concerned with the problems of death and consolation. The theory of immortality in this philosophy is expressed by saying that when death occurs, you take away the mirror—but the rose is still there. This image seems to me a very powerful one. It's not the same as the Christian idea of the soul, of course, but it emphasizes the thing I want to talk about, which is that you can't dissociate the person from the world he lives and functions in and that you can somehow measure the person by the degree of his involvement in that world. The soul is not contained *within* the body but outside, in the theater of its commitments.

The most precise expression of this idea that I know of in our literature is by a famous English poet. I want to quote it because it says something rather nicely about the relationship of two human beings, and the great It, the world. This is in *Troilus and Cressida*, where *It* is a famous Hellenic enterprise. There was a time when Achilles was having some difficulties about the siege of Troy and people were trying to buck him up. At one point Ulysses comes on. It's part of the play where nothing much is going to happen for a few minutes. Sometimes in Shakespeare when nothing is going to happen, you have an exchange of bawdy jokes for the boys in the pit and sometimes you have a bit of relevant philosophizing. In the play this bit of philosophizing is relevant to Ulysses' effort to goad Achilles into action; but it has a universal relevance as well:

Ulysses   A strange fellow here
    Writes me that man—how dearly ever parted,
    How much in having, or without or in—

Cannot make boast to have that which he hath,
Nor feels not what he owes, but by reflection;
As when his virtues shining upon others
Heat them, and they retort that heat again
To the first giver.

Achilles   This is not strange, Ulysses
The beauty that is borne here in the face
The bearer knows not, but commends itself
To others' eyes; nor doth the eye itself—
That most pure spirit of sense—behold itself,
Not going from itself; but eye to eye opposed
Salutes each other with each other's form;
For speculation turns not to itself
Till it hath travell'd and is mirror'd there
Where it may see itself. This is not strange at all.

Ulysses   I do not strain at the position—
It is familiar—but at the author's drift;
Who, in his circumstance, expressly proves
That no man is the lord of anything—
Though in and of him there be much consisting—
Till he communicate his parts to others.
Nor doth he of himself know them for aught
Till he behold them formed in th'applause
Where th'are extended; who, like an arch, reverb'rate
The voice again or, like a gate of steel
Fronting the sun, receives and renders back
His figure and his heat.

(Tudor Text, Players Edition, Collins)

No Ajax, no Achilles even, can *be* the lord of anything, much less *know* his own worth, save through resonance with others engrossed in those same matters. No child, I wish to say, can gain competence and knowledge, or know himself as competent and as a knower, save through communication with others involved with him in his enterprises. Without a Thou, there is no I evolving. Without an It there is no content for the context, no figure and no heat, but only an affair of mirrors confronting each other.

Children are members of the same species as adults, but they are also quite a distinct subspecies and we want to be careful about not exaggerating the differences and not forgetting them, either. It seems clear to me that there are many complicated, difficult things they learn or can learn, and such learning occurs in an environment where there are other human beings who serve, so to speak, as a part of the learning process. Long before there were such things as schools, which are rather recent institutions in the history of our kind, there were teachers. There were adults who lived in the village and who responded to the signals that children know very well how to emit in order to get attention from adults. These adults managed, quite spontaneously and without benefit of the theory of instruction, to be teachers.

I really need a kind of electronic analogy here for what goes on in a child's mind. Think of circuits that have to be completed. Signals go out along one bundle of channels, something happens, and signals come back along another bundle of channels; and there's some sort of feedback involved. Children are not always able to sort out all of this feedback for themselves. The adult's function, in the child's learning, is to provide a kind of external loop, to provide a selective feedback from the child's own choice and action. The child's involvement gets some response from an adult and this in turn is made available to the child. The child is learning about himself through his joint effects on the non-human *and* the human world around him.

The function of the teacher, then, is to respond diagnostically and helpfully to a child's behavior, to make what he considers to be an appropriate response, a response which the child needs to complete the process he's engaged in at a given moment. Now, this function of the teacher isn't going to go on forever: it's going to terminate at some time in the future. What we can say, I think, and what we clearly ought to provide for, is that the child should learn how to internalize the function which the adult has been providing. So, in a sense, you become educated when you become your own teacher. If being educated meant no longer needing a teacher—a definition I would recommend—it would mean that you had been presented with models of teaching, or people playing this external role, and that you have learned how the role was played and how to play it for yourself. At that point you would declare your independence of instruction as such and you would be your own teacher. What we all hope, of course, is that as the formal, institutional part of education is finished, its most conspicuous and valuable product will be seen to be the child's ability to educate himself. If this doesn't happen, it doesn't make sense to say that the processes we try to initiate in school are going to be carried on when people leave school.

The image I want, then, is really the image Shakespeare is working with. You grow as a human being by the incorporation of conjoint information from the natural world *and* of things which only other human beings are able to provide for in your education.

I sometimes think that working in the style we like to work in—which is much farther along in English primary schools, I'm sorry to say, than in American schools—we forget the unique importance of the human role. We tend to say "Oh well, if children just have a good rich, manipulable and responsive environment, then everything will take care of itself." When you visit a class which is operating in this way, with a teacher who has a good bag of tricks, you're often impressed that the teacher doesn't seem to be very necessary. He can leave the room and nobody notices it. If *you* don't have that bag of tricks, you always rather marvel at what goes into it. After everything is accomplished it all looks as though it's very spontaneous. But, of course, that's a dangerous illusion. It's true only in those periods—in good schools frequent periods—when children don't need the external loop. When they do need it and there's no one around to contribute the adult resonance, then they're not always able to carry on the process of investigation, of inquiry and exploration, of learning, because they need help over a hump that they can't surmount through their own resources. If help isn't available, the inquiry will taper off, and that particular episode, at least, will have failed to accomplish what it otherwise might have.

Now, I'm speaking as one very much in favor of richness and diversity in the environment, and of teaching which allows a group of children to diversify their activities and which—far more than we usually think proper—keeps out of their hair. What seems very clear to me—and I think this is a descriptive, factual statement, not praising or blaming—is that if you operate a school, as we in America almost entirely do, in such a style that the children are rather passively sitting in neat rows and columns and manipulating you into believing that they're being attentive because they're not making any trouble, then you won't get very much information about them. Not getting much information about them, you won't be a very good diagnostician of what they need. Not being a good diagnostician, you will be a poor teacher.

The child's overt involvement in a rather self-directed way, using the big muscles and not just the small ones, is most important to the teacher in providing an input of information wide in range and variety. It is input which potentially has much more heft than what you can possibly get from the merely verbal or written responses of a child to questions put to him or tasks set for him. When we fail in this diagnostic role we begin to worry about "assessment."

I think this is fairly obvious. It doesn't say that you *will* but that you *can* get more significant diagnostic information about children, and can refine your behavior as a teacher far beyond the point of what's possible when every child is being made to perform in a rather uniform pattern. But of course you will not get the information, or will not use it, if you are just sweetly permissive and limp, if you don't provide the external feedback loop when you think it is needed. We know children never do behave uniformly even when they're supposed to. When it appears they are, it's just because they've learned the trick of pleasing you—or displeasing you if they're all on strike!—and then you aren't able to make the needed discrimination.

But I think the real importance of teacher intervention comes out in situations where a child is not involved in very many things, is not responsive to anything you provide. That child may be a problem; that child who doesn't give you much information, who is tight and constrained, often called "good." But you get little suggestions or inklings of interest and involvement, you get hunches about what might prove absorbing to him. If you have enough of these hunches and enough persistence you find *something* that works and when you do you have laid the basis for a new relationship between yourself and that child, and this is the thing that is really important.

The rest is good and important and not too hard to describe: when children are being diverse in what they're doing, selective in what they're doing; when you're giving them genuine alternatives—then you are bound to get much more knowledge of them from reading the language of their behavior. Of course, you certainly aren't going to succeed all the time with every child in this diagnostic and planning process. There are going to be several misses for every hit, but you just say, "Well, let's keep on missing and the more we miss the more we'll hit." The importance of this in the "I–Thou" relationship between the teacher and the child is that the child learns something about the adult which we can describe with words like "confidence," "trust" and "respect."

You have done something for the child which he could not do for himself, and he knows it. He's become involved in something new which has proved engrossing to him. If he thus learns that he has a competence he didn't know he had, then you have been a very crucial figure in his life. You have provided that external loop, that external feedback, which he couldn't provide for himself. He then values the provisioner with the provision.

What is the feeling you have toward a person who does this for you? It needn't be what we call love, but it certainly *is* what we call respect. You value another person because he is uniquely useful to you in helping you on with your own life. "Love" is, perhaps, a perfectly good word, too, but it has a great variety of meanings and has been vulgarized, not least by psychological theory.

The relationship that develops with different children will be different just because they are different children. When *you* give a child a range from which to make choices, the choices *he* makes in turn give you the basis for deciding what should be done next, what the provisioning should be for him. That is *your* decision, it's dependent on *your* goals, it's something *you* are responsible for—not in an authoritarian way but you do have to make a decision and it's your decision, not the child's. If it's a decision to let him alone you are just as responsible for it as if it's a decision to intervene.

The investment in the child's life that is made in this way by the adult, the teacher in this case, is something that adds to and in a way transforms the interest the child develops spontaneously. If, as sometimes happens, a child gets particularly interested in a variation on a soap bubble theme that you've already given him, you can just happen to put nearby some other things that might not at first seem related to soap bubbles—some geometrical wire cubes, tetrahedra, helices, and wire with a soldering iron. The resulting soap films are almost bound to catch the fancy of many human beings, including children. What have they got? Well, they've got a certain formal geometrical elegance, they've got color: when you look at the films in the right kind of light you see all those marvelous interference colors. Such a trap is bristling with invitations and questions. Some children will sample it and walk on; but some will be hooked by it, will get very involved with it. Now, this kind of involvement is terribly important, I think. It's aesthetic, or it's mathematical, or it's scientific. It's all of these potentially, and none of them exclusively. The teacher has made possible this

SECTION THREE

96 ....

relation between the child and "It," even if this is just by having "It" in the room; and for the child even this brings the teacher as a person, a "Thou," into the picture. For the child this is not merely something which is fun to play with, which is exciting and colorful and has associations with many other sorts of things in his experience: it's also a basis for communication with the teacher on a new level, and with a new dignity.

Until the child is going on his own the teacher can't treat him as a person who is going on his own, cannot let him be mirrored there, where he may see himself as investigator or craftsman. Until he is an autonomous human being who is thinking his own thoughts and making his own unique, individual kinds of self-expression out of them, there isn't anything for the teacher to respect, except a potentiality. So the first act in teaching, it seems to me, the first goal, necessary to all others, is to encourage this kind of engrossment. Then the child comes alive for the teacher as well as the teacher for the child. They have a common theme for discussion; they are involved together in the world.

I had always been awkward in certain kinds of situations with young children. I didn't know them very well and I'd sort of forgotten that I'd once been one, as we mostly do. I remember being very impressed by the way some people, in an encounter with a young child, would seem automatically to gain acceptance while other people, in apparently very friendly encounters with the same child, would produce real withdrawal and, if they persisted, fear and even terror. Such was the well-meaning adult who wanted to befriend the child—I and Thou— in a vacuum. It's traumatic, and I think we all know what it feels like. I came to realize (I learned with a good teacher) that one of the very important factors in this kind of situation is that there be some third thing which is of interest to the child *and* to the adult, in which they can join in outward projection. Only this creates a possible stable bond of communication, of shared concern.

My most self-conscious experience of this kind of thing was when a few years ago I found myself with two very small tykes who had gone with me and my wife to the hospital to get their mother, who had just had a third baby. The father was ill and there was already some anxiety. With Frances Hawkins they were fine; indeed it was she who had earlier been my teacher in this art. They were perfectly happy with us two but they had never been with me alone. Suddenly the nurse announced in a firm voice that children could not go beyond this point, so my wife had to go in and we three had to stay. It was one of those moments when you could have had a fairly lively scene on your hands. Not being an adept, I thought quite consciously of the triangular principle. There had to be some third thing that wasn't I and the two children, otherwise we were all going to be laid waste. And there wasn't anything! I looked around and there was a bare hospital corridor. But on one wall there was a collection of photographs of some recent banquet that had been given for a donor, so in desperation I just picked them up, rushed over to it, and said, "Look!" That's a sort of confession, because I'm sure many of you would know how to handle this kind of situation: for me it was a great triumph and it was a demonstration, if an oddly mechanical one, of a consciously held principle. And it worked.

It seems to me that this kind of episode, which is in itself trivial and superficial, can symbolize a lot that is important in terms of the teacher-child relationship; namely, the common interest, the common involvement in subject-matter. Now of course, you never really deceive a child in important matters, so this interest can't long be feigned, as it was in my story. If you don't find something interesting, and try to feign an interest you don't have, the investment won't last. But if there is that common interest it may last and may evolve. You need to be capable of noticing what the child's eyes notice and capable of interpreting the words and acts by which he tries to communicate with you. It may not be in adult English, so the reception of these signals requires experience and close attention.

Visualize a long transparent corked plastic tube with water and other things in it, as fancy may dictate. Many years ago I would have thought that this was rather trivial, rather silly, and would have said, "What's there to be learned from that?" To tell you the truth, I honestly still don't know, there is so much! We can use a lot of words in physics that have something to do with it; or we can talk about color and motion and other things of some aesthetic importance. By now I've seen enough children involved in this particular curious apparatus to be quite convinced that there's a great deal in it—and I don't mean just this particular tube but many similar artifacts, as well as samples of the natural world. Such things can serve as an extraordinary kind of bond. The child is in some sense functioning to incorporate the world; he's trying to assimilate his environment. This includes his social environment, of course, but it also includes the inanimate environment; it also includes the resources of the daily world around him, which he's capable of seeing for the most part with far fresher eyes than ours. The richer this adult-provided contact, therefore, the more firm is the bond that is established between the human beings who are involved.

Finally, I'd like to mention something which is perhaps of special interest and which takes me into psychological theory. It has to do with how human beings come to attain the sense of objectivity, the sense of reality, with how they come to get a stable, reliable vision of the world around them and how, without losing their capacity for fantasy, they are able to make clear discriminations between what they know, what they have learned, what they merely believe, what they imagine, and so on. It has to do with how they are able to get straight the orders and kinds of belief and credibility. This is one of the most important accomplishments of a human being.

It seems to me that for some children and not for others this capacity for fitting things together into a coherent whole, into a coherent pattern, comes first mostly in terms of their relations with the human world, while for other children it comes first mostly in their relations with the inanimate world.

The capacity for synthesis, for building a stable framework within which many episodes of experience can be put together coherently, comes with the transition from autistic behavior to exploratory behavior. The first is guided by a schedule which is surely inborn, and is connected with satisfaction of definite infant needs. The second has a different style, and is not purposive in the same way, not aimed at a predetermined end-state. Its satisfaction, its reinforcement as a way of functioning, comes along the way and not at the end; in competence acquired, not in satiation. Both modes of behavior are elaborated through experience, but exploratory behavior is not bound and limited by a schedule of needs—needs which must, to begin with, have the highest priority. A child's first major synthetic achievements in exploratory learning may come in relation to the human world, but they may come equally, and perhaps more readily, in his exploration of the things of his surrounding physical environment, and of their responsiveness to his testing and trying. In either case, or so it seems to me, the exploratory motivation, and its reinforcement, is of a different kind from the libidinous, aimed as the latter is at incorporation and possession. And the child's development will be limited and distorted if it does not, by turns, explore *both* the personal and the non-personal aspects of his environment; but explore them, not exploit them for a known end. Most psychologists, in my reading and my more extensive arguing with them, tend to say that the roots of human motivation are interpersonal. They say that the fundamental dynamics of the child's relation to the rest of the world as he grows up stem from his relation to his mother, his relation to other close figures around him, and that these will be the impelling forces in his life. It is, of course, in such terms that Freud built up his whole systematic theory and although perhaps there aren't many very orthodox Freudians around nowadays this key feature of the theory persists, I think—the feeling that the only important formative things in life are other human beings. And if people pay attention to the non-human world—it may include animals and plants as well as the physical environment, enriched to contain bubble tubes and soap film—one tends to trace this to some desire to exploit the human world: for example, the child does something because he thinks it pleases you or because he thinks it displeases you, or because he's escaping you—but never because he wants wholeheartedly to do what he's doing. In other words, there's been a systematic tendency to devalue children's thing-oriented interests as against their person-oriented interests. It is assumed that the latter are basic, the former derivative. All I would like to say is that I think the interest in *things* is a perfectly real, perfectly independent and autonomous interest which is there in young children just as genuinely as the interest in persons is there. And some children are *only* able to develop humanly by first coming to grips in an exploratory and involved way with the inanimate world.

We've certainly seen examples of children who very early have got on to the tricks which I suppose in some sense babies are born with but which infants can elaborate as they grow older, tricks for getting what they want from persons by planning how they shall behave. It's exploiting, and some very young children are already skillful at it. If you know such children as a teacher you'll know they're smarter than you are because they've put a lot more investment into this kind of thing than you have. You have to be very shrewd to cope with them.

One thing such a child cannot do is to get wholeheartedly involved in anything else; he has to be watching all the time to see what the adults and the other children think about it. But if you can set enough traps for him, if you can keep exposing him to temptations, if he sees other children involved and not paying any attention to the teacher, he's left out in the cold. So the temptations of bubbles or clay or sand or whatever it is are reinforced by the fact that other children aren't playing his kind of game. If such a child once forgets his game, because he *does* get involved in shaping some inanimate raw material, in something that's just there to be explored, played with, investigated, tried out, then he has had an experience which is liberating, that can free him from the kind of game-playing which he's got so expert at. He comes, after all, from a species that is called *homo faber.* If he doesn't get free of manipulating persons somewhere in his life, that life is going to be a sad one. In the extreme case perhaps it will even be a psychotic one. Children of this extreme sort are a special case, but being extreme, in a way they tell us a lot about what is involved in the three-cornered relationship of my title. They seek to get and to keep, but cannot yet even begin to give. For the verb *to give* has two objects and only the indirect one is personal. The direct object must be something treasured which is not I, and not Thou.

One final remark. It seems to me that many of us, whether our background was in science or not, have learned something about ourselves from working with children in this way that we've begun to explore. We've begun to see the things of the physical and biological world through children's eyes rather more than we were able to before, and have discovered and enjoyed a lot that is there that we were not aware of before. We don't any longer feel satisfied with the kind of adult grasp that we had of the very subject matter that we've been teaching; we find it more problematic, more full of surprises, and less and less a matter of the textbook order.

One of the nicest stories of this kind that I know comes from a young physicist friend who was very learned. He had just got his Ph.D. and of course he understood everything. (The Ph.D. has been called "the certificate of omniscience.") My wife was asking him to explain something to her about two coupled pendulums. He said, "Well, now, you can see that there's a conservation of . . . Well, there's really a conservation of angle here." She looked at him. "Well, you see, in the transfer of energy from one pendulum to the other there is . . ." and so on and so on. And she said, "No, I don't mean that, I want you to notice this and tell me what's happening." Finally, he looked at the pendulums and he saw what she was asking. He looked at *it*, and he looked at *her*, and he grinned and said, "Well, I know the right words but I don't understand it either." This confession, wrung from a potential teacher, I've always valued very much. It proves that we're all in *it* together.

This essay raises some important questions about teaching (e.g., When should I intervene? Do I still have control of this discussion?). John Mason considers decision making about teaching a temporary resolution of tensions among alternative choices. For him, teaching is full of these adjustments and teachers are therefore plagued by uncertainty. This is both the best and worst aspect of teaching. Best, because there is always another decision and another chance to fine-tune one's teaching. Worst, because one is never done, never "correct," and there are no guidelines for making the best decisions.

You may confront many of the tensions he identifies. Is control an issue because you and the principal have different ideas about the value of a quiet classroom? Do you have to submit the results of a unit test on fractions to the math supervisor before spring break? When your students meet in small discussion groups, are you uncertain about what they are learning? It can be a relief to read that you are not alone in struggling with these questions.

Tensions*

John Mason

Have you ever had the experience, in the middle of a lesson, of suddenly wishing you were not there? Like a wave washing over you, you realise that things are not going well. Perhaps you "take control" and conduct things from the blackboard; perhaps you "let them keep working," waiting for the bell to ring. The feeling of inadequacy, but of having to cope, is an example of a tension.

Have you ever found yourself talking, telling students things, and wished that somehow things were different, that *they* were doing the work? Or have you ever got a group of students talking, and having heard how inarticulate they are, how little they understand, wished that you had never embarked in this direction? This is an example of a tension.

Like elastic bands wound up, feelings of inadequacy or guilt, or just knots in the stomach are indications that you have touched a basic tension. Another way to detect tensions is to notice "if onlys."

- If only students wanted to learn . . .
- If only they would pay attention . . .
- If only the class were smaller . . .

These too are indicators of underlying tensions. Despite the fact that "if only" implies that things could be different, they do not actually go away when the ideal conditions are achieved, they just surface in a new guise. Yet each day these tensions *are* coped with in some fashion by

* Originally published in *Mathematics Teaching*, 114 (March 1986): 28–31. It is an edited version of a lecture to the 11th conference of the Australian Association of Mathematics Teachers in Brisbane, January 1986.

each and every teacher. Some stance, some action is taken, which often obscures the underlying dilemma.

The resultant of all the many forces on teachers is often, not surprisingly, inaction and numbness. In this article, I want to acknowledge openly a number of tensions that I experience, and which I suspect others may recognise. I do this in the belief that by admitting them publicly we will discover that others share them. The history of education in general, and mathematics education in particular, is riddled with attempts to nullify basic tensions. Yet I suspect most tensions are endemic and inescapable. Getting them out into the open means that they can be robbed of their numbing effect, and turned instead into potent sources of energy.

Consider the following quotes from students and teachers:

> The students asked me if "this was on the exam." I said, "Well, no, not exactly . . ." and they switched off immediately.

> I want to get them enjoying mathematics. They just want to get through the day.

> Don't make me think about it, just tell me how to do it!

> I've read the card Miss, but is it an add or a multiply?

These are the sorts of remarks that are heard quite often, signalling the presence of a basic tension of teaching and learning. In what follows I have tried to be explicit and specific about experiences which are by their nature woolly and indeterminate, resisting expression. Looking back over them, I see that in many cases the same underlying tension is addressed in different ways.

Keeping Control

I must keep my class under control, both to permit individuals to work, and so as not to disturb other classes.

> With a new class I want the students to feel that I am in control and that I know what I'm doing. I tend to keep a tight rein at first, and gradually relax as I get to know them.

The stronger my control, the less opportunity for individuals to explore, to express their own ideas. Yet inevitably there are one or two pupils who do not seem to respond to my way of working, who are hard to control.

> The only question is how to survive to the end of the lesson. If I turn my back, then some of them immediately start break-dancing round the room!

Do other teachers have similar difficulties? New teachers on probation may be afraid to admit to difficulties, for fear of being branded inadequate, and even losing their job. An experienced teacher may be wary of revealing uncertainties for fear of losing status in the eyes of colleagues, or perhaps the chance of promotion.

> If I work the way I want to, what will the teacher think who takes them next year?

A head of department may be too concerned with gaining or keeping the respect of colleagues to admit to having problems.

Time

The syllabus is packed, the examination looms, there is too little time to cover all the material. If I stop and get the students discussing, or investigating, I will lose valuable time, and some topic will be missed.

The tension of time is unresolvable, no matter how it is approached, due to the pressures of society to "get on." If I take the time necessary for students to really understand a topic, then I will certainly have trouble exposing them to everything that is expected. On the other hand, I might be able to demonstrate, even inculcate, ways of thinking that will enable them to take on new topics much more quickly.

Notice how discussion of lack of sufficient time brings up some standard primitives and metaphors:

> I was afraid we wouldn't get there/reach the topic.

> I felt I had to push a bit harder to get to the answer in the lesson.

The metaphor of "knowledge as place," and of "teaching as movement" is quite common. Is it appropriate? A related metaphor is revealed in expressions such as

There isn't time to cover the syllabus.

I haven't covered inequalities yet.

Painting seems to be a popular pastime—but is it an appropriate image? What images might be more accurate or more precise?

Shortage of time is a common complaint in every walk of life, but perhaps it is only a perception. If I really want to do something, I will find the time. Put another way, perhaps the things I do with my time *are* really what I want to do.

Confidence v Challenge

It has been said over and over again that students need to gain confidence, and that confidence comes from success. Unfortunately, success is associated only with jumping hurdles, like tests and examinations, and not also with seeing a generality, or capturing it in words and symbols, or explaining it to someone else. The result is that we try to "give students confidence" by providing simple tasks with little or no challenge.

For example, the current concern about "low attainers" stems directly from the requirement that all students study mathematics every year, but indirectly from the age-old observation that "standards are falling." (Cicero complained bitterly of this, and was by no means the first!) The confidence–challenge tension leads educators to simplify the tasks given to low-attaining students, to break things down into tiny anodyne steps. An intellectual challenge is removed on the grounds that they cannot handle it, and so all edge, all interest, is gone.

Product v Process

I want my students to participate in mathematical thinking, and to take the initiative. I know that *their* actual task is to pass the examinations they meet. *Their* attention is on learning what they are told they have to learn, on being able to do the questions. *My* wish is to emphasize thinking skills so that they will be able to deal with unexpected questions on an examination, and more importantly, continue thinking and questioning throughout their lives. As soon as I start "teaching" mathematical processes, there is a real danger that they will simply become products, words to be memorised.

For example, I want my students to realise deeply within themselves that it often helps to specialise—to try simple cases, systematically as well as randomly—and then to generalise—to look for a general pattern. But how long do I let them struggle with a complicated example before intervening? If I come in too quickly, specialising will become a superficial behaviour, and it will not be available as a potent force when they really need it. If I give no clues, they may never become aware of the power of specialising.

> Students will quickly learn to say the "right" words back to you,
> but do they really appreciate their real meaning?

This dilemma is endemic. The way we cope depends on many factors, such as whether the particular answer really matters or whether it is being used as a vehicle to introduce, or work on, "specialising." Frustration is important in mathematics, for you cannot really experience release, that beautiful sense of things falling into place, if you have not previously been confused, feeling that things were out of place.

Analogously, you cannot guide trainee teachers past the fundamental teacher tensions. They have to experience the dilemmas themselves before they can ever "hear" the advice. It is an old story; but there is no royal road to learning (or teaching).

Autonomy

Students need standards against which to measure their own performance. The more the standards are imposed by the teacher, the more the students are "working for their teacher," rather than for themselves. In primary and early secondary school there may appear to be no harm done, but when students get older and disaffected with school, their teachers become part of "the system." Students may lose their reason for working unless they have learned to work for themselves, to value the pleasure that comes with seeing, and with being able to explain to others.

What then do I do with a capable but unproductive student? Some forceful pushing may help get through a barrier, but it may also produce dependency on me to keep pushing. If the teacher imposes all the discipline, then will the students learn to access their own will, or do they simply bide their time until they leave school? If a teacher leaves it up to the students to work on their own initiative, will they miss out on essential skills while coming to grips with being responsible for their own learning? When they are stuck, it is so much more attractive to tell them what I think than to encourage and cajole them to tell me what they think. It also gives me pleasure to rehearse a story clearly that I have thought about. It reinforces my "seeing." Unfortunately it also reduces their opportunity to "see." For me, Gattegno's memorable expression "the subordination of teaching to learning" sums up this tension. To teach, to take the initiative, to impose what shall be attended to, puts the student in the position of reacting to external pressure. Military disciplinarians believe that by imposing very strong discipline you break through barriers and train people to be highly self-disciplined. Some students take to it, others reject it as soon as possible. At the other extreme, I can elect to work with and respond to those who give evidence of wishing to work mathematically, and simply keep some semblance of order amongst the rest. Some may "take advantage" of this way of acting, and not discover until too late what they were missing.

There is no answer to this tension, no way to relieve it. I can decide how I am going to act, stick to my guns, and ignore the consequences. I can also keep alive inside me an awareness of the delicate balance, looking out for an opportunity to support independent initiative within whatever restrictions are imposed. What *is* important is being alive to the tension, rather than trying to avoid it.

Intervening

The tensions mentioned so far are fairly global. There are also many more specific ones felt moment to moment in the classroom. For example, a group of students are "working" at a table. Should I intervene? How? Why? Shall I let them carry on and see for themselves; shall I "guide" or "direct" them? Must I be present for something worthwhile to happen?

Must I check that everything is correct? What if they go away with a misunderstanding? (When don't they?!) In any group there are liable to be passengers. Does it matter? What should I do? How can I tell if someone is actually working, or just copying?

A standard way to intervene with one or more students is to ask them something along the lines of "tell me what you're doing." Another way to intervene is silently, simply listening to what they are saying, and watching what they are writing. Some students don't like being watched, however.

Sometimes an intervention provides a useful impetus to try to articulate what they are doing and, in the process, see things more clearly for themselves. Sometimes an intervention blocks progress. Just when the struggle is most important, my intervention may draw students back to earlier parts of their investigation, perhaps even exposing unsuspected or overlooked difficulties, and leave them feeling that they are getting nowhere.

If I am working on student autonomy, then I have to find some way to remind students that it often helps to talk out loud to someone, and to establish an atmosphere in which they readily approach each other and me for this purpose.

Didactic Contract

The didactic contract is between teacher and student, although it may never be made explicit. The teacher's task is to foster learning, but it is the student who must do the learning. The student's task is to learn, or at least to get through the system. They wish to be told what they need to know, and often they wish to invest a minimum of energy in order to succeed. Guy Brousseau, who coined the expression "didactic contract," points out that it contains a paradoxical dilemma. Acceding to the student's perspective reduces the potential for the student to learn, yet the teacher's task is to establish conditions to help the student learn. But what does it mean to learn, and how is it best assisted? The teacher looks for certain telltale behaviour, as does the examiner. The student seeks to provide that behaviour. Soon the focus is on the behaviour, not on the inner state which gives rise to behaviour. The dilemma is then that everything the teacher does to make the student produce the behaviour the teacher expects, tends to deprive the student of the conditions necessary for producing the behaviour as a byproduct of learning; the behaviour sought and the behaviour produced become the focus of attention.

Put another way, the more the teacher is explicit about what behaviour is wanted, the less opportunity the students have to come to it for themselves and make the underlying knowledge or understanding their own. Thus for example, if I want students to understand subtraction, the more *I* rehearse different details of the algorithm publicly, the less likely the student is to do anything other than pick up the outer show. If I want students to become aware of a generality, the more I guide them, the less chance they have of really appreciating it for themselves.

The dilemma is not even as simple as this, because under certain conditions, exactly what I need is to see someone else going through the steps, or to have my behaviour confirmed, or to hear the generality articulated.

Students have many different views as to the nature of learning and the role of teachers, and part of the work with a new class is in some cases to get them to modify their perspective. William Perry has brilliantly charted the development of different perspectives amongst college students: he has described a number of "positions," which vary from

- My teacher knows the truth and is responsible for telling it to me clearly.
- In some areas there is certainty, and, in some, only opinion backed up by reasoning: my job is to learn how to justify my opinions, and to examine critically those of others.

Certainly many of the "Perry positions" are visible in staff-rooms as well as playgrounds. To stay alive as a teacher, it is necessary to be aware of the variety of perspectives and that they are very deep rooted.

In the midst of a lesson we have to cope, so we respond to the pressures of the moment. But I have also caught myself locking up energy in resentment or guilt or "if onlys." I experience a struggle between

- What I can do.
- What I think I ought to do, what I think others do, what I want to do.

I believe that it is important to be open to these sorts of dilemmas, to take opportunities to talk about them with colleagues, to try to become precise in our articulations, because then it is possible to unlock the blocked energy and exploit it positively.

Vivian Gussin Paley is a highly reflective teacher. She tape-records her classroom and spends a great deal of time thinking about her teaching and her young students' learning. Inquiry is an integral part of her planning and teaching; the curiosity she exhibits is vital. Here Paley traces her growing curiosity about young children's thought and shows vividly the importance of listening to children. She also describes the process she uses to record and reflect on what her students are saying.

Paley is the author of many books on early childhood learning. The vignettes she includes in them are helpful stimuli for analyzing children's thinking.

On Listening to What the Children Say*

Vivian Gussin Paley

Years ago, when I was a young woman in New Orleans, I led a Great Books discussion group that met at the public library. The participants came from many occupations and educational backgrounds, and they were all older and more experienced than I. Whatever advantage I had was contained in the lists of questions provided by the Great Books people, who also sent along the following directive: There are no right or wrong answers. Get everyone talking and then find connections—person-to-person, person-to-book.

The advice was sound: do the required reading, ask most of the questions, and manage to connect a number of the ideas that arise at each meeting. Unfortunately, I did not fare too well; something was missing from my performance—a simple ingredient called *curiosity*. I was not truly interested in the people sitting around the table or curious about what they might think or say. Mainly, I wanted to keep the discussion moving and to avoid awkward silences.

Soon after leading these discussions, I became a kindergarten teacher. In my haste to supply the children with my own bits and pieces of neatly labeled reality, the appearance of a correct answer gave me the surest feeling that I was teaching. Curriculum guides replaced the lists of questions, but I still wanted most of all to keep things moving with a minimum of distraction. It did not occur to me that the distractions might be the sounds of children thinking.

Then one year a high school science teacher asked if he could

* Originally published in *Harvard Educational Review* 56 (2): 122–131. May 1986.

spend some time with my kindergartners. His first grandchild was about to enter nursery school, and he wondered what it would be like to teach the youngest students in our school. Once a week he came with paper bags full of show-and-tell, and he and the children talked about a wide range of ordinary phenomena. As I listened, distant memories stirred. "You have a remarkable way with children, Bill." I told him. "They never tire of giving you their ideas, and somehow you manage to use them all, no matter how far off the mark."

"The old Socratic method," he said. "I was a Great Books leader once up in Maine. It seems to work as well with kindergartners as with my seniors."

Of course. That was exactly what he was doing. He asked a question or made a casual observation, then repeated each child's comment and hung onto it until a link was made to someone else's idea. Together they were constructing a paper chain of magical imaginings mixed with some solid facts, and Bill was providing the glue.

But something else was going on that was essential to Bill's success. He was truly curious. He had few expectations of what five-year-olds might say or think, and he listened to their responses with the anticipation one brings to the theater when a mystery is being revealed. Bill was interested not in what he knew to be an answer, but only in how the children intuitively approached a problem. He would whisper to me after each session, "Incredible! Their notions of cause and effect are incredible!" And I, their teacher, who thought I knew the children so well, was often equally astonished.

I began to copy Bill's style whenever the children and I had formal discussions. I practiced his open-ended questions, the kind that seek no specific answers but rather build a chain of ideas without the need for closure. It was not easy. I felt myself always waiting for the right answer—my answer. The children knew I was waiting and watched my face for clues. Clearly, it was not enough simply to copy someone else's teaching manner; real change comes about only through the painful recognition of one's own vulnerability.

A move to a new school in another city and an orientation speech given by Philip Jackson shook me up sufficiently to allow the first rays of self-awareness to seep in. He described a remarkable study done by two Harvard psychologists, Robert Rosenthal and Lenore Jacobson, who deliberately supplied several teachers with misleading information about their students.[1] In random fashion, children were labeled bright or slow by means of fictitious IQ scores. The teachers, I was shocked to find out, consistently asked more questions, waited longer for answers, and followed up more often with additional comments when they were speaking to a "smart" child.

I was shocked because I knew that one of those unsuspecting teachers could have been me, although certainly I listened more to myself than to *any* of the children in the classroom. Suddenly, I was truly curious about my role in the classroom, but there were no researchers ready to set up an incriminating study to show me when—and perhaps why—I consistently veered away from the child's agenda. Then I discovered the tape recorder and knew, after transcribing the first tape, that I could become my own best witness.

The tape recorder, with its unrelenting fidelity, captured the unheard or unfinished murmur, the misunderstood and mystifying context, the disembodied voices asking for clarification and comfort. It also captured the impatience in *my* voice as children struggled for attention, approval, and justice. The tape recordings created for me an overwhelming need to know more about the process of teaching and learning and about my own classroom as a unique society to be studied.

The act of teaching became a daily search for the child's point of view accompanied by the sometimes unwelcome disclosure of my hidden attitudes. The search was what mattered—only later did someone tell me it was research—and it provided an open-ended script from which to observe, interpret, and integrate the living drama of the classroom.

I began using the tape recorder to try to figure out why the children were lively and imaginative in certain discussions, yet fidgety and distracted in others ("Are you almost finished now, teacher?"), wanting to return quickly to their interrupted play. As I transcribed the daily tapes, several phenomena emerged. Whenever the discussion touched on fantasy, fairness, or friendship ("the three Fs" I began to call them), participation zoomed upward. If the topic concerned, for example, what to do when all the blocks are used up before you can build something or when your best friend won't let you play in her spaceship, attention would be riveted on this and other related problems: Is it fair that Paul always gets to be Luke Skywalker and Ben has to be the bad guy? And, speaking of bad guys, why should the wolf be allowed to eat up the first two pigs? Can't the three pigs just stay home with their mother?

These were urgent questions, and passion made the children eloquent. They reached to the outer limits of their verbal and mental abilities in order to argue, explain, and persuade. No one moved to end the discussion until Justice and Reason prevailed.

After the discussion, a second, more obvious truth emerged. If the tape recorder was left running, what I replayed later and dutifully transcribed became a source of increasing fascination for me. The subjects that inspired our best discussions were the same ones that occupied most of the free play. The children sounded like groups of actors, rehearsing spontaneous skits on a moving stage, blending into one another's plots, carrying on philosophical debates while borrowing freely from the fragments of dialogue that floated by. Themes from fairy tales and television cartoons mixed easily with social commentary and private fantasies, so that what to me often sounded random and erratic formed a familiar and comfortable world for the children.

In fact, the children were continually making natural connections, adding a structure of rules and traditions according to their own logic. They reinvented and explained the codes of behavior every time they talked and played, each child attempting in some way to answer the question, What is going on in this place called school, and what role do I play?

"Let's pretend" was a stronger glue than any preplanned list of topics, and the need to make friends, assuage jealousy, and gain a sense of one's own destiny provided better reasons for self-control than all my disciplinary devices. A different reality coexisted beside my own, containing more vitality, originality, and wide-open potential than could be found in any lesson plan. How was I to enter this intriguing place, and toward what end would the children's play become my work?

The tape recorder revealed that I had already joined the play. I heard myself always as part of the scene, approving, disapproving, reacting to, being reacted to. The question was not *how* would I enter but, rather, *what* were the effects of my intervention? When did my words lead the children to think and say more about their problems and possibilities, and when did my words circumvent the issue and silence the actors? When did my answers close the subject?

Once again, the decisive factor for me was curiosity. When my intention was limited to announcing my own point of view, communication came to a halt. My voice drowned out the children's. However, when they said things that surprised me, exposing ideas I did not imagine they held, my excitement mounted and I could feel myself transcribing their words even as they spoke. I kept the children talking, savoring the uniqueness of responses so singularly different from mine. The rules of teaching had changed; I now wanted to hear the answers I could not myself invent. IQ scores were irrelevant in the realms of fantasy, friendship, and fairness where every child could reach into a deep well-spring of opinions and images. Indeed, the inventions tumbled out as if they simply had been waiting for me to stop talking and begin listening.

Later, teaching at a nursery school, I found that the unanticipated explanations of younger children bloomed in even greater profusion. The crosscurrents of partially overheard talk lifted my curiosity to new heights. It was similar to watching the instant replay of an exciting baseball moment. Did the runner really touch second base? Did Frederick actually say, "My mother doesn't have no more birthdays"? What does a four-year-old mean by this odd statement made in the doll corner? The next day I am pressed to find out.

> "Frederick, I'm curious about something I heard you say in the doll corner yesterday. You said your mother doesn't have birthdays any more." (Frederick knows my tendency to begin informal conversations in this manner, and he responds immediately.)
>
> "She doesn't. How I know is no one comes to her birthday and she doesn't make the cake."
>
> "Do you mean she doesn't have a birthday *party*?"
>
> "No. She really doesn't have a *birthday*."
>
> "Does she still get older every year?"
>
> "I think so. You know how much old she is? Twenty-two."
>
> "Maybe you and your dad could make her a birthday party."
>
> "But they never remember her birthday and when it's her birthday they forget when her birthday comes, and when her birthday comes they forget how old she is because they never put any candles. So how can we say how she is old?"
>
> "The candles tell you how old someone is?"
>
> "You can't be old if you don't have candles."
>
> "Frederick, I'll tell you a good thing to do. Ask mother to have a cake and candles. Then she'll tell you when her birthday is."
>
> "No. Because, see, she doesn't have a mother so she doesn't have a birthday."
>
> "You think because your grandma died your mother won't have any more birthdays?"

"Right. Because, see, my grandma borned her once upon a time. Then she told her about her birthday. Then every time she had a birthday my grandma told. So she knew how many candles to be old."

I turn to Mollie. "Frederick says his mother doesn't have any more birthdays."

"Why doesn't she?" Mollie wants to know.

"Because," Frederick answers patiently, "because my grandma died and my mother doesn't know how many candles old she is."

"Oh. Did your grandfather died, too?"

"Yeah. But he came back alive again."

Mollie stares solemnly at Frederick. "Then your grandma told him. If he whispers it to your mother maybe it's already her birthday today."

"Why should he whisper, Mollie?" I ask.

"If it's a secret," she says.

"I think Mollie has a good idea, Frederick. Why don't you ask your grandfather?"

"Okay. I'll tell him if my mommy could have a birthday on that day that they told her it was her birthday."

Why not just tell Frederick the truth: "*Of course* your mother has a birthday; everyone has a birthday." Tempting as it might be to set the record straight, I have discovered that I can't seem to teach the children that which they don't already know.

I had, in fact, made this very statement—that everyone has a birthday—the previous week in another context. I had brought a special snack to school to celebrate my own birthday, and Frederick and Mollie seemed surprised.

"Why?" they asked.

"Why did I bring the cookies?"

"Why is it your birthday?"

"But everyone has a birthday. Today happens to be mine."

"Why *is* it your birthday?" Mollie insisted, attempting to give more meaning to her question by emphasizing another word.

"Well, I was born on this day a long time ago."

The conversation ended and we ate the cookies, but clearly nothing was settled. Their premises and mine did not match. What, for instance, could it possibly mean to be born on *this* day a long time ago?

A week later, Frederick made cause and effect out of the presence of one's own mother and the occasion of a birthday. The matter is not unimportant, because the phenomenon of the birthday looms large. It is constantly being turned around and viewed from every angle, as are the acts of going to bed, going to work, cooking meals, shooting bad guys, calling the doctor or the babysitter—to name just a few of the Great Ideas present in the preschool.

Every day someone, somewhere in the room, plays out a version of "birthday." Birthday cakes are made of playdough and sand, and it is Superman's birthday or Care Bear's birthday or Mollie's birthday. "Birthday" is a curriculum in itself. Besides being a study in numbers, age, birth, and death, it provides an ongoing opportunity to explore the three Fs—fantasy, friendship, and fairness.

"You can't come to my birthday if you say that!"

"You *could* come to my birthday, and my daddy will give you a hundred pieces of gum if you let me see your Gobot."

Any serious observation made about a birthday is worth following up, not in order to give Frederick the facts and close the subject, but to use this compelling material as a vehicle for examining his ideas of how the world works. If I am to know Frederick, I must understand, among many other things, how he perceives his mother's birthday and his grandfather's permanence.

As the year progresses I will pick up the threads of these and other misconceptions and inventions in his play, his conversation, his storytelling, and his responses to books and poems. He will make connections that weave in and out of imagined and real events, and I will let my curiosity accompany his own as he discards old stories and creates new ones.

My samples of dialogue are from the kindergarten and nursery school, the classes I teach. But the goal is the same, no matter what the age of the student; someone must be there to listen, respond, and add a dab of glue to the important words that burst forth.

The key is curiosity, and it is curiosity, not answers, that we model. As we seek to learn more about a child, we demonstrate the acts of observing, listening, questioning, and wondering. When we are curious about a child's words and our responses to those words, the child feels respected. The child *is* respected. "What are these ideas I have that are so interesting to the teacher? I must be somebody with good ideas."

Children who know others are listening may begin to listen to themselves, and if the teacher acts as the tape recorder, they may one day become their own critics.

Reading between the lines is both easier and harder when the setting is preschool. It is easier because young children rehearse their lines over and over in social play and private monologues, without self-consciousness; older children have already learned to fear exposing their uncommon ideas. On the other hand, the young child continually operates from unexpected premises. The older student's thinking is closer to an adult's and easier to fathom: the inevitability of birthdays is not an issue in the third grade, and the causal relationship between age and candles has long since been solved. Yet, third graders and high school students struggle with their own set of confusions, fantasies, and opinions that need to be listened to, studied, compared, and connected.

The fact that the thoughts of the teacher and student are furthest apart in preschool makes it a fruitful place for research and practice in the art of listening to what children say and trying to figure out what they mean. My curiosity keeps me there, for I still cannot predict what children of three and four will say and do. One must listen to them over long periods of time. Being their teacher provides me the rare luxury of living with my subjects for two years. Like a slow-motion Polaroid developing its images, piece by piece, over many months, the children's patterns of thought and speech need much time to be revealed.

An early conversation with a group of three-year-olds convinced me that these were the children who would best prove my assumption that the first order of reality in the classroom is the student's point of view, for here the pathways to knowledge lead directly through the doll corner and the building blocks. For me this is where the lessons are to be found.

> Carrie has her own version of hide-and-seek, in which she pretends to hide and pretends to seek. She hides a favorite possession, then asks a teacher to help her find it. She pretends to look for it as she takes the teacher directly to the missing item. "Oh, here's my dolly's brush!" she squeals delightedly. All these games resist the unknown and the possibility of loss. They are designed to give the child control in the most direct way.
>
> Sometimes, however, the child has no control; something is really missing. Then the threes are likely to approach the problem

as if the question is "What is *not* missing?" This is exactly what happens when I try to direct the children's attention to an empty space in the playground. Over the weekend, an unsafe climbing structure has been removed. The doll corner window overlooks the area that housed the rickety old frame.

"See if you can tell what's missing from our playground?" I ask.

"The sandbox."

"The squirrely tree."

"The slide."

"But I can *see* all those things. They're still in the playground. Something else was there, something very big, and now it's gone."

"The boat."

"Mollie, look. There's the boat. I'm talking about a big, brown, wooden thing that was right there where my finger is pointing."

"Because there's too much dirt."

"But what was on top of the place where there's too much dirt?"

"It could be grass. You could plant grass."

Libby and Samantha, four-year-olds, see us crowded around the window and walk over to investigate. "Where's the climbing house?" Libby asks. "Someone stoled the climbing house."

"No one stole the house, Libby. We asked some men to take it down for us. Remember how shaky it was? We were afraid somebody would fall."

The threes continue staring, confused. I should have anticipated their response and urged that the structure be dismantled during school hours.[2]

If my words contain more stories than theories, it may be that I have taken on the young child's perspective, which seems to be organized around the imperative of *story*. I am still listening to what the children say, but since the younger children disclose more of themselves as characters in a story than as participants in a discussion, I must now follow the plot as carefully as the dialogue. School begins to make sense to the children when they pretend it is something else. And teaching, in a way, makes sense to me when I pretend the classroom is a stage and we are all actors telling our stories.

We do more than tell our stories; we also act them out. The formal storytelling and acting that often arise out of and run parallel to the children's fantasy play have become a central feature of our day. The children's stories form the perfect middle ground between the children and me, for they enable us to speak to one another in the same language.

Much to my surprise, when I moved from the kindergarten to the nursery school, I found that the storytelling and acting were accepted with equal enthusiasm as the natural order, for nearly everything there takes on more recognizable shape in fantasy.

> If, in the world of fantasy play, four- and five-year-olds may be called characters in search of a plot, then the three-year-old is surely a character in search of a character.
> Place this three-year-old in a room with other threes, and sooner or later they will become an acting company. Should there happen to be a number of somewhat older peers about to offer stage directions and dialogue, the metamorphosis will come sooner rather than later. The dramatic images that flutter through their minds, as so many unbound stream-of-consciousness novels, begin to emerge as audible scripts to be performed on demand.[3]

Possibilities for connecting play and outside events are fleeting, but the teacher who listens carefully has many opportunities to apply the glue. In the following episode, Mollie joins the older girls for a pretend valentine party in the doll corner. Here the play is more real to her than the actual event to come. My task is to help Mollie connect the doll corner reality to the classroom celebration—quite different from the usual procedure of connecting *my* reality to a classroom celebration. This is the doll corner version of the holiday.

> "Ding-dong. Ring-ring."
> "Come in. Who is it?"
> "Trick or treat valentine."
> "Don't say trick or treat to our house. The baby is sleeping. Don't ring the bell."
> "I'm making valentines for the baby. 'I love you.' This spells 'I love you.' "
> "Teacher, can you write 'I love you' on my baby valentines? This is my valentine to get married and have a baby. This is Valentine's Day."
> "Are you having a valentine party?" I ask Mollie.
> "It's the baby's birthday valentine. I'm giving everyone whoever is nice a valentine."
> When Valentine's Day arrives Mollie is surprised that her picture valentines are meant to be given away.
> "But Mollie, that's why your mother bought them. You're supposed to give one to each child."

"No, it's for me." Mollie insists, starting to cry. "It says M-O-L-L-I-E."

"Mother wrote your name so the children will know they're from you."

She cries vigorously. "I have to bring them home. My mommy said."

"Okay, Mollie. Let's put them back in the box."

Instantly the tears stop. "I'm telling a valentine story and it has a monkey climbed a tree. Then he fell down on a cushion. Then another monkey came."

"Which is the part about Valentine's Day?"

"The part about the monkey climbed a tree." Mollie looks at her box of valentines, then at the table filled with lacy red hearts. Today's event is controlled by others; she can think only of a monkey climbing a tree.

The image of the doll corner valentine party suddenly fills my mind and I gather the children around me. "I have a valentine story for us to act out. Once upon a time there was a valentine family with a mother, father, sister, brother, and baby. They were all busy making valentines because it was Valentine's Day and the baby's birthday also. "We have to write 'I love you' and give them to all the nice animals who ring our bell," they said. Ring-ring. Who is it? It's the four bears. Good. Here's your valentines. Ring-ring. Who is it? It's the four squirrels. Oh, good. Here's your valentines. Ring-ring. Who is it? It's the four elephants. Oh, very good. Here's your valentines. Ring-ring. Who is it? It's the four rabbits. Oh, very, very good. Here's your valentines. And all you animals must bring your valentines to the baby's birthday valentine party."

Mollie jumps up. "Wait a minute. I'm the sister. I have to get my valentines. I'm supposed to give them to the animals."

Mollie has an entree into the holiday. Moments earlier she was an outsider, just as she was, in fact, to school itself during the first few weeks. She worked her way to an understanding of school through the same doll corner fantasies that now illuminate Valentine's Day. And I, the outsider to three-year-old thinking, am learning to listen at the doll corner doorway for the sounds of reality.[4]

A month later, Mollie tells her own valentine story. "Once a time the valentines came to a little girl that was Fire Star. It was her birthday that day they came. Her real birthday."

"And was it also the real Valentine's Day?" I ask.

"It *was* the real valentine's birthday and also the real Fire Star and also the pretend Fire Star."

Mollie struggles with the idea of a real and pretend Fire Star. She will attempt to explain this enigma to herself and others as she acts it out, and my questions will not always be of help. Often, in fact, my questions fall flat or add to the confusion. At such times, my expectations and those of the children may be too far apart—or the children *think* they are too far apart.

The children cannot always figure out the adults' relation to fantasy play. What powers do we possess that might affect the outcome? Can we, for instance, hear the children's thoughts?

"Why is Leslie doing that?" Mollie asks me. Leslie is her baby sister.

"Doing what?" I ask.

"Crying in my head. Did you listen?"

"Mollie, I can't hear the sounds in your head," I reply.

"Margaret, can you hear Leslie crying in my head?" Mollie asks.

"Yeah, I hear her crying in your house," Margaret says.

"She wants milk from her mama, that's why," Mollie informs her.

"I already knew that," Margaret nods.

I must have misread the question. Did Mollie want me to imagine that Leslie was crying? What do the children think about adults' literal approach to events? . . . Such is the concern, I think, when I unexpectedly appear at the door of the doll corner during a hospital drama.

"Come here, nurse," Libby says impatiently to Mollie. "Come here and undress the baby."

"Are you the mother?" Mollie asks.

"Yes, and Peter is the doctor. I'm sick too. Hurry, put the medicine on me. I cut my knee. Put on the stitches, doctor. Look in my mouth. Say you see bumps. Put us in the x-ray."

"Sh! There's the teacher." Mollie points to me as I pass by. "What if she calls this the doll corner?"

"She can't see us. We're in the hospital. It's far away downtown."

"Sh! She'll think it's the doll corner."

"Get inside the hospital. We're getting far away so she doesn't know where the hospital is."[5]

The vivid image of her sister crying and the equally graphic hospital scene present Mollie with a similar worry. Does the teacher understand the nature of the fantasy and, if not, to what extent do the fantasy and its players exist? When Mollie was two, she did not perceive the boundaries of these internal pictures; by the time she is six, she will know what can be seen and heard by others. But now she may sometimes flounder in doubt between her reality and mine.

So often I drift around on the edge of their knowing without finding a place to land. Here, for example, is a peanut butter and jelly tale that continues to perplex me.

> Of the eight children at my snack table, six ask for peanut butter and jelly on their crackers, one wants plain peanut butter, and one, plain jelly. My question: What did I make more of, peanut butter and jelly or plain peanut butter? The children stare at me blankly and no one answers.
>
> "What I mean is, did more people ask for peanut butter and jelly or did more want plain peanut butter?" Silence. "I'll count the children who are eating peanut butter and jelly." I count to six. "And only Barney has peanut butter."
>
> "Because Barney likes peanut butter," Mollie explains.
>
> "Yes, but did I make more sandwiches that have both peanut butter and jelly?"
>
> "Because we like peanut butter *and* jelly," Frederick responds patiently.
>
> My question has misfired again and this time I can imagine several possible reasons. Since everyone is eating peanut butter and/or jelly, the entire group is included in the peanut butter and jelly category. In addition, "more" could refer to those who asked for more than one sandwich. Perhaps the word "plain" is the stumbling block or they may think I want to know why they chose peanut butter with or without jelly.
>
> Another possibility: Peanut butter and jelly may be akin to Peter and the Wolf, in that the words are not easily separated. Thus, "peanut butter and jelly" also represents plain peanut butter or plain jelly.
>
> . . . I anticipate the obvious response, but the children do not follow my thinking. Perhaps at another time they might have accidently linked their images to mine. Of one thing I am certain: had I put my inquiries into dramatic form and given us roles to play, I would have been understood.[6]

Tomorrow we *will* act it out, but probably not with peanut butter and jelly. Images tend to stay fixed for a long time in the young child's mind. No matter. The proper message has come across: confusion—

mine or theirs—is as natural a condition as clarity. The natural response to confusion is to keep trying to connect what you already know to what you don't know.

Next time the children and I may be on the same track, and meanwhile we are getting valuable practice in sending signals. As anyone who attends the theater knows, clues and signals are given all along the way, but the answers are never revealed in the first act. The classroom has all the elements of theater, and the observant, self-examining teacher will not need a drama critic to uncover character, plot, and meaning. We are, all of us, the actors trying to find the meaning of the scenes in which we find ourselves. The scripts are not yet fully written, so we must listen with curiosity and great care to the main characters who are, of course, the children.

Notes

1. Rosenthal, R. and L. Jacobson. 1968. *Pygmalion in the Classroom: Teacher Expectations and Pupils' Intellectual Development*. New York: Holt, Rinehart & Winston.

2. Vivan Gussin Paley. 1986. *Mollie Is Three*. Chicago, University of Chicago Press, pp. 69–70.

3. Paley, *Mollie Is Three*, p. xvi.

4. Paley, *Mollie Is Three*, pp. 92–94.

5. Paley, *Mollie Is Three*, pp. 102–103.

6. Paley, *Mollie Is Three*, pp. 91–92.

With the new emphasis on mathematics as communication, many teachers want to learn how to ask questions that support children's discussions. Peter Sullivan offers clear starting points that are adaptable to all curriculums and classrooms. He poses questions that encourage rich investigations and sets out the principles behind constructing them.

As you read this selection, you might want to recall questions that generate rich mathematical talk in your classroom and think about the characteristics they share.

Improving the Quality of Learning by Asking "Good" Questions*

Peter Sullivan

Introduction

The first chapter of this monograph examined the important role which questions play in communication between teachers and pupils. It is argued that the quality and type of questions are directly related to the quality and type of learning. In particular, it seems that questions which require the pupils to think more deeply are likely to produce better learning outcomes than questions for which pupils need only remember a fact or a routine. Unfortunately there are no easy ways to identify questions which are accessible to the majority of pupils and which also require higher levels of thinking. This chapter discusses a type of question which has the potential to stimulate higher levels of thinking using everyday mathematics content and which can be attempted satisfactorily by most pupils.

Consider the following example. One particular Year 6 pupil, Jane, had just completed a unit on measurement, the final aspect of which was on calculating perimeter and area. The class had been set a task which included diagrams of rectangles with dimensions given. The pupils were asked to calculate the perimeter and area. Jane was able to complete these items correctly. However, in a subsequent discussion, when asked the question:

* Originally published in P. Sullivan & D. Clarke, *Communication in the Classroom: The Importance of Good Questioning*. Geelong, Victoria, Australia: Deakin University Press. 1991.

> A rectangle has a perimeter of 30 units. What might be its area?

the pupil could not answer and in fact claimed that there was insufficient information. The question clearly requires a different level of thinking from standard text exercises on perimeter and area. To find one or more answers which satisfy the conditions a pupil must think about the constraints which the perimeter of 30 places on the lengths of the sides of the rectangle, as well as thinking about the area. In terms of the earlier discussion, it is a higher order question.

Now it is recognised that this particular question is complex in a number of ways. Firstly, the language could have created a problem. In this case, the teacher was able to discuss the question with Jane and she appeared to be able to restate the question in her own words. Secondly, it is framed in an unfamiliar way. This may well have caused some confusion. In particular, pupils find it difficult to cope with mathematics questions which have more than one correct answer. Phrases such as "might be" give such questions a speculative tone which some pupils may consider out of place in a mathematics question. This may well have been the basis of Jane's difficulties. After experience with such questions this may not be a serious problem.

Notwithstanding these factors, the question did allow the teacher to assess the learning of Jane on this topic in a different way. It had appeared from the test that Jane had mastered the topic since she could accurately complete the exercises on perimeter and area. After further probing it was revealed that Jane had very little appreciation of perimeter as the distance around, and she had no concept of area as covering. In other words, she learned to answer routine exercises but had not fully understood the concepts. This question enabled the teacher to become aware of the depth of Jane's understanding on this topic. Another feature of the question was that it became clear to Jane that her understanding of the concepts was inadequate.

This chapter describes how questions can be identified or constructed which require a higher level of thinking about mathematics content, and which require the use of problem-solving skills. These questions can provide similar information over a range of topics to help teachers to assess pupils' understanding better and to provide a clearer appreciation of the quality of the learning both for the teacher and the pupils themselves. Such questions are called, for the purpose of this discussion, "good" questions. "Good" questions are defined as possessing three features:

1. They require *more than recall* of a fact or reproduction of a skill.
2. *Pupils can learn by doing the task*, and the teacher learns about the pupil from the attempt.
3. There may be *several acceptable answers*.

Each of these features is discussed in the following sections.

More Than Recall

Bloom et al. (1969) claimed that levels of thinking included knowledge, comprehension, application, analysis, synthesis and evaluation. While there has been much debate about the application of these to classroom teaching, they serve as a useful guide in this instance. It is unfortunate that much mathematics teaching simply requires pupils to recall some knowledge or to reproduce a skill. Few of the exercises which appear in the major mathematics texts in primary or secondary mathematics require much analysis, synthesis or evaluation. Even exercises which allow the possibility of the levels termed comprehension and application are often completed by recalling a set procedure (Desforges & Cockburn 1987).

The above question on perimeter and area required comprehension of the task, application of the concepts and appropriate skills, and analysis and some synthesis of the two major components involved. Yet it must be stressed that the question was not a trick, nor did it require the processing of complex information. The unfamiliarity of the context could have caused some difficulties. Jane may not have had experience with tasks which required such levels of thinking. In this case some caution was necessary in interpreting Jane's inability to respond. It is possible that if Jane had had some experience with questions with more than one possible answer she may have found some of the solutions. It is also desirable that pupils gain experience in exercising the higher levels of thinking. Jane may well have had little or no experience at answering questions which required analysis and synthesis of information. Questions like the one above have the potential to provide such experiences.

Another example of this type of question is on the topic of averages. A common question in textbooks takes the form "Find the average of 12.3, 13.71, 13.5, 20.2 and 16.7." This requires mainly recall of a technique. If the question is asked as follows:

The average of five numbers is 17.2. What might the numbers be?

it requires a different level of thinking and a different type of understanding of the topic of averages to be able to give an answer which satisfies both the teacher and the pupil. Pupils need both to comprehend and analyse the task. In this case, they must have a clear indication of the concept of average and must either use the principle that the scores are evenly placed about the average or that the total of the scores is five times 17.2 (86.0) as the basis of their response. It is more than recall.

Pupils Can Learn by Doing the Task

Socrates apparently believed that he could teach anything through the use of carefully selected questions. In a much quoted example, he guided a slave to deduce the length of the side of a square of area 8 square units from the information that a square of side 2 has an area of 4 square units. The assertion is that a person can be led to such a conclusion without any direct instruction, by drawing on their existing knowledge, through judicious questioning. "This knowledge will not come from teaching but from questioning. He will recover it for himself" (Plato 1956, p. 138). In other words, the pupil can learn from the act of answering the question. "Good" questions are particularly suitable for this.

Consider the following question:

John and Maria each measured the length of the basketball court. John said that it was 20 rulers long, and Maria said that it was 19½ rulers long. How could this happen?

The authors asked some upper primary pupils to discuss the question in groups. The pupils suggested a variety of plausible explanations.

Based on their explanations, the pupils were invited to suggest what they need to think about when measuring length. Their list included:

- The need to agree on levels of accuracy;
- The need to agree on where to start and finish, and the importance of starting at the zero;
- The need to avoid overlap at the ends of the rulers, or spaces between the ends;
- The need to measure in a straight line; and
- The need to measure the shortest (perpendicular) distance.

It is in this sense that the pupils learnt by doing the task. In this example, the pupils were able to establish for themselves these essential aspects of measurement from the act of answering the question.

Another component of learning from the question itself is that pupils can become more aware of what they know, and what they do not know. At times the learners' knowledge may be inappropriate or incomplete. The task of the teacher in such instances is to make the pupils aware of their own incomplete understanding of the concept and to assist them to become aware of the need to adapt their understanding to accommodate new information. It is what Bell (1982) called "provoking conflicts and exposing misconceptions" (p. 11).

In the earlier question on finding the area of a shape with perimeter 30 units, the conflict arises by requiring the pupil to consider both perimeter and area together. By thinking about perimeter and area at the same time the pupil is made aware of the fact that the area can change even though the perimeter is fixed. In this sense, the very act of trying to complete the question can help the learners to gain a better understanding of the concepts of perimeter and area.

Several Acceptable Answers

As has been suggested above, most questions in mathematics classes have only one correct answer. There is nothing wrong with such questions, but there are also many mathematical situations where there is a range of possible alternatives. Pupils should experience such possibilities at times.

Consider the following example:

> A basketballer scored 11 points in three games. What might be her scores in each of the games?

Clearly there are many possible answers to the question. It entails no additional knowledge than an addition task of the type $3 + 4 + 4 = ?$, yet it requires a different approach and a different level of thinking as well as revealing to the pupils that multiple correct answers are possible.

There also appears to be a link between such questions and fostering higher level thinking. Sweller, Mawer and Ward (1983) showed that the use of open-ended questions develops student's problem-solving expertise while still meeting the conventional goals of mathematical skill acquisition. Under Sweller's instructional model the conventional task, "Find the sum of these two numbers," would be modified by the new requirement, "Find out everything you can." For example:

> Find out everything you can about these three numbers: 9, 16, 25

Note that there are different levels of sophistication at which individual pupils might respond. It is characteristic of such "good" questions that each pupil can make a valid response which reflects the extent of the pupil's understanding. A pupil with a broad understanding of the topic can be expected to make more general statements. Since correct answers can be provided at a number of levels, such tasks are particularly appropriate for mixed ability classes. For example, a pupil who responds quickly at a superficial level can be asked to search for alternative or more general solutions. Able students will typically recognise the possibility of such alternatives for themselves and devote the same time and effort in the search for a general solution that less able students expend on a less sophisticated solution. This is discussed further in the next chapter.

In the case of the earlier question on the area of the rectangle, there is a range of acceptable answers, even using only whole number lengths ($14 \times 1, \ldots 8 \times 7$). Some pupils might be asked to find the largest possible area. It might be suggested to others that they draw a graph. Some pupils will recognise that an adequate answer might require the identification of a class of suitable rectangles. Pupils can even be asked to describe all possible rectangles. It is the openness of the task which provides this richness. It is the existence of several acceptable answers which stimulates the higher level thinking. The need to devise a method or solution rather than recalling a routine characterises both "good" questions and mathematical problem solving generally.

How to Construct Good Questions

It is possible for teachers to make up their own "good" questions for their own year level and for the content they intend the pupils to learn. However it is not something that can be done "on your feet." It is necessary to plan the questions beforehand. It goes without saying that questions must be pitched at the appropriate level for the class. The teacher is the best judge of this. In many cases the questions can be placed after most aspects of the topic have already been taught. There are also examples which are suitable as an introduction. These decisions belong to the teacher.

Two methods which teachers can use to construct "good" questions are presented in Figures A and B. Each can be used for most topics and for any level. You are invited to try to construct some "good" questions for your teaching in the near future.

Summary and Conclusion

The quality of the learning of pupils is related to the quality of communication with the teacher, an important component of which is the questions that the teacher asks. This chapter has presented examples of a type of question which has the potential to stimulate higher order thinking in the pupils.

It is suggested that the quality of learning can be improved by asking questions which require more than recall of information by the pupils, from which the pupils can learn by the act of answering the question, and which allow for a range of possible answers. These are called "good" questions. Other features of "good" questions are:

- They should be clear.
- All pupils should be able to make a start.
- The responses make it clear to both pupil and teacher when the pupil's learning is incomplete, possibly by provoking a conflict with existing conceptions.

Method 1   Working backwards

This is a three-step process.

Step 1   Identify a topic (tomorrow's class?).
Step 2   Think of an answer.
Step 3   Make up a question which includes (or addresses) the answer.

For example:

Step 1 Identify a topic	**Step 2** Think of an answer	**Step 3** Make up a question which includes the answer
Rounding	5.8	What numbers could be rounded off to 5.8?
Counting	4 chairs	What is there in the room that there are 4 of?
Graphing		What could this be a graph of?
Area	12 sq cm	Draw a triangle with an area of 12 sq. cm.
Percentages	30%	30% of the pupils in a school play basketball. How many pupils might there be in the school and how many play basketball?
Fractions	3½	Two numbers are multiplied to give 3½. What might the numbers be?
Money	36 cents	I went to the shop and got 36 cents change. What did I buy and how much did it cost?

FIG. A

Method 2 Adapting a standard question

This method is also a three-step process.

Step 1   Identify the topic.
Step 2   Think of a standard question.
Step 3   Adapt it to make a good question.

For example:

Step 1 Identify the topic	**Step 2** Think of a standard question	**Step 3** Adapt it to make a "good" question
Length	Measure your table using handspans.	What is there in the room which is three handspans long?
Geometry	What is a square?	Write down everything you can about this square.
Addition	337 + 456 =	What might the missing numbers be? 3__7 + __6 = 53__
Subtraction	371 – 256 _____ ____	Fill in the missing numbers: ____ – ____ _____ 371
Averages	Find the average height of three students.	The average height of three students is 145 cm. If you are one of the students, who might be the other two?

FIG. B

- Pupils with clear understandings will be able to solve the task efficiently, and it will be obvious to both teacher and pupil that they have.
- There will be potential for further investigation to challenge and extend those students with thorough understandings.

It is noted that the use of such questions makes specific demands on the teacher. As well as being receptive to all pupil responses, the teacher must acknowledge the validity of the various responses while making clear any limitations, drawing out contradictions or misconceptions, and building class discussion from partial answers. The questions provide the environment for better learning; it is up to the teacher to ensure that the opportunities for learning become realities. It is possible to construct such questions for most topics and levels. Suggested techniques are to work backwards from the answers and to adapt standard questions. The potential exists to stimulate higher order thinking by the pupils and to improve the quality of their understandings as a result.

References

Bell, A. 1982. "Treating student misconceptions." *Australian Mathematics Teacher* 38(3): 11–14.

Bloom, B., M. Englehart, E. Furst, W. Hill & C. Krathwohl. 1969. *Taxonomy of Educational Objectives*. New York: David McKay Co.

Desforges, C. & A. Cockburn. 1987. *Understanding the Mathematics Teacher: A Study of Practice in First Schools*. New York: David McKay Co.

Plato. 1956. *Protagoras and Meno*, trans. W. K. C. Guthrie. London: Penguin Classics.

Sweller, J., R. F. Mawer & M. R. Ward. 1983. "Development of expertise in mathematical problem solving." *Journal of Experimental Psychology: General* 112(4): 639–61.

Marion Walter is an inspiration to many mathematics teachers. She discovers excellent problems embedded in a variety of everyday situations and models ways of capitalizing on children's curiosity, persistence, and excitement. Student involvement in investigations often depends on the problem that is posed; selecting problems is sometimes a difficult task.

Here she writes about the characteristics of good mathematics problems and describes some that produce good talk, multiple solutions, exploratory questions, and a variety of representations. Walter also considers ways of responding to student-posed problems. You may find problems here to try out in your classroom.

Curriculum Topics Through Problem Posing*

Marion Walter
Mathematics Department, University of Oregon

Problem *solving* has received much attention in the past years and younger children are beginning to be seriously involved in it. Problem *posing* is beginning to receive attention and it, too, can begin in the earlier years. Furthermore, if we encourage students to engage in problem posing, we can involve them more deeply in the development of topics that we wish *to cover;* in fact, we can use problem posing to help students *uncover* mathematics.

Addition Problems

Students are often presented with pages of addition problems. What message does this give to the students? Surely one message is that they are not capable of making up their own practice problems. (I realise of course the advantage of giving students all the same problems—it is easier to check the answers!) What might one do instead and why?

Suppose the students are just beginning to learn how to add three digit numbers and that they have just worked out:

* Originally published in *Mathematics Teaching* 128 (September 1989): 23–25. Parts of this article include material presented at the 1989 ATM Easter Course at St. Martin's, Lancaster.

$$
\begin{array}{r}
3\ 4\ 2 \\
+\ 5\ 3\ 4 \\
\hline
\end{array}
$$

where there is no need to regroup or "carry." If we ask them to make up more such exercises, they will soon be faced with the challenge of what numbers to choose so that the total in each column is less than 10 if they wish to avoid having to regroup. Surely this would be a learning situation.

Or, suppose they are given:

$$
\begin{array}{r}
3\ 4\ 2 \\
+\ 2\ 1\ 8 \\
\hline
\end{array}
$$

might it not be worthwhile to challenge the students to make up some more problems where the units column adds up to ten?

Or, let's turn the task around. Given:

$$
\begin{array}{r}
3\ 4\ 2 \\
+\ 5\ 3\ 4 \\
\hline
\end{array}
$$

what problems can you or your students pose?

One technique of problem posing just asks you to look at the given, in this case an addition problem, and asks you or your students to try to think of other problems. Stephen Brown and I have called this *accepting the given* (Brown & Walter 1983), and we sometimes call it *brute force* problem posing. Among the suggestions from participants at Lancaster, using only this technique of problem posing, were:

> Here the answer is 876. Make up other addition problems of two 3-digit numbers whose sum is 876. What do you think students will be discovering or learning if they do this?
>
> Make up other 3-digit addition problems whose answers consist of three consecutive digits.
>
> Rearrange the digits of each 3-digit number in 342 + 534 to get the largest possible total.
>
> Find all the different totals you can get by rearranging the digits.
>
> Make up a story that goes with 342 + 534.
>
> Make up other 3-digit problems for which the answer is such

that the digit in the tens place is one greater than the digit in the units place.

Notice that each of these problems can raise or lead to other problems. For example, the second raises the additional problem: *what are all possible 3-digit numbers that consist of consecutive integers?* And what about the totals of 876 and 678? Can one always or ever reverse the digits of the addends to get the reversed total?

$$\begin{array}{r} 3\,1\,2 \\ +\,5\,6\,4 \\ \hline 8\,7\,6 \end{array} \quad \text{and} \quad \begin{array}{r} 2\,1\,3 \\ +\,4\,6\,5 \\ \hline 6\,7\,8 \end{array}$$

but
$$\begin{array}{r} 3\,5\,9 \\ +\,5\,1\,7 \\ \hline 8\,7\,6 \end{array} \quad \begin{array}{r} 9\,5\,3 \\ +\,7\,1\,5 \\ \hline 1\,6\,6\,8 \end{array} \quad \begin{array}{r} 1\,3\,7 \\ +\,7\,3\,9 \\ \hline 8\,7\,6 \end{array} \quad \begin{array}{r} 7\,3\,1 \\ +\,9\,3\,7 \\ \hline 1\,6\,6\,8 \end{array}$$

If it is not possible, will one always get 1668 instead of 678? Explore.

The fourth problem might give rise to the question: *how many different totals are there?*

You will think of many other problems even without using any other techniques of problem posing. In this way students can be engaged in problem posing and problem solving while also getting practice in addition. Students will be thinking and will be involved in creating their own problems. Thus at an early age they can experience some mathematics in the making. They can learn from experience that mathematics is *not* a subject in which you have to be told everything and memorise a lot.

Fractions

Next, I suggested a fraction exercise as a starting point: *what problems can you think of when faced with ⅔ + ⅕?*

Usually students are given such problems, and they either have learned the algorithm for finding the answer or they make mistakes. They are usually not asked to think.

Among some interesting problems that were posed at Lancaster were these two:

When in real life would you ever have to add these two
fractions?
How many different ways can you add these?

Some questions one might pose and which I posed to the group are:

Which is bigger, ⅔ or ⅕?
Is the answer less or more than 1?
By how much does ⅔ differ from 1?
By how much does ⅕ differ from 1?
What must one add to ⅔ + ⅕ to obtain a total of 1?

I had worked this last question out and found: ⅔ + ⅕ + ²⁄₁₅ = 1.
Using Polya's admonition, which he so often said in his class: *Look
at the problem,* I noticed that one could get the answer ²⁄₁₅ by multi-
plying the numerators and denominators of ⅔ and ⅕. I had chosen ⅔
+ ⅕ at random when I wrote it down on an overhead some time before
Lancaster and had calculated the ²⁄₁₅. I was lucky! This immediately
raised the question: *What other fractions could one start with so that
one could find the right answer by this "wrong" method?* This is such
a rich problem that I have since "milked" it a great deal (Borasi 1986).

Geometric Figure

Next I took a geometric starting point: a regular hexagon.
Instead of beginning with what one wants "to teach" about a
regular hexagon, (what does one want students to know about a regular
hexagon anyway?), let us brute force problem pose. Here are some of
the problems and questions that were suggested by the group:

How many diagonals does it have?
How many triangles can you make?

Note that this is a good example of a question that would need to be
clarified by students. This is a valuable activity because it is misleading to
always give clearly stated and well defined problems and learning to
clarify problems is in itself a worthwhile activity.

When all the diagonals are drawn in, how many regions are
   formed?
What is the length of each diagonal? Or one might ask, how
   many different lengths are there?
What is the area of the hexagon formed by joining the alternate
   vertices?
What is the largest circle you can draw in it?
If it is not rigid, what shapes can you deform it into?

I suggested one of my favorite questions: *can you construct a
regular hexagon, not only by using straightedge and compass, but
from a paper circle, or a rectangle, or a scrap of paper or an equilateral
triangle?* (Walter 1981).
   If we draw diagrams suggested by some of the questions above,
or other simple diagrams using a regular hexagon as a starting point,
many more questions are suggested (see Figure A). Perhaps you want
to pose a few now.

Other Starting Points

We briefly examined 3x = 12 as a starting point (Walter 1988), as well
as the problem of how many different triangles one could construct out
of a stick of length 10 cm if each side has to be a whole number of
centimeters and the stick gets used up each time one triangle is made.
This is a nice problem that really brings home the triangle inequality—
the sum of two sides of a triangle is greater than the third side. Warning:
No easy formula exists that tells you how many triangles are possible
for sticks of length n cm (Jordan et al. 1979).

Group Work

Part of the time was spent by participants in small groups choosing
their own starting points—ones useful for the curriculum items they
have "to cover." Since there were teachers of all levels from infant to
upper secondary, we got a variety of topics, ranging from a delightfully
rich one that started with the dustbin to a trigonometry one: $\sin^2 x +
\cos^2 x = 1$.
   The group discussing the dustbin (see Figure B) created many
wonderful questions including:

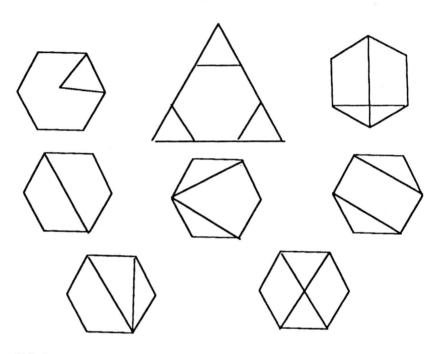

FIG. A

How many dustbins are needed to collect the week's school
    litter?
How high is it?
What else can you measure about this dustbin?
How many ways can you fit the lid on the bin?
Is it better to have two little bins or one big one?
What do you think would fit in this bin—an elephant? a
    bird . . . ?
Find the volume of the dustbin.
If the bin is half full of water, how high is the water level?
How much bigger is the top rim than the bottom one?
What else can you use it for? Would it be useful for storing
    toys?
What if you could not reach into the bottom?
What else can you put the rubbish in—what are some
    attributes of a good rubbish holder?

FIG. B

I believe the teacher who suggested this starting point had done a whole chunk of curriculum around the rubbish bin! After listing several questions suggested by $\sin^2 x + \cos^2 x = 1$, I pondered on how often we "teach" this without expressing the wonder about how special it is. Can we say anything about $\sin(x) + \cos(x)$, for example, or $\sin^2 x - \cos^2 x$ or $\tan(x) + \sin(x)$?

I do not have a record of the work of the other groups at Lancaster, but I hope that even this small report will encourage others to engage in problem posing while trying to "cover" the curriculum.

References

Borasi, R. 1986. "Algebraic Explorations of the Error $^{16}/_{64} = ^1/_4$." *Mathematics Teacher* (April): 246–48. Wrong methods that give the right answers have been discussed in many places by several authors. R. Borasi has written much about it. I am not sure yet where the further discussion of the problem will be published.

Brown, S. & M. Walter. 1983. *The Art of Problem Posing.* Hillsdale, NJ: Lawrence Erlbaum.

Jordan, J. H., et al. 1979. "Triangles with Integer Sides." *American Mathematical Monthly* 86 (8): 686–89.

Walter, M. 1981. "Are We Robbing Our Students of a Chance to Learn?" *For the Learning of Mathematics* 1 (3).

———. 1988. "Some Roles of Problem Posing in the Learning of Mathematics." In *Mathematics, Teachers and Children*, ed. D. Pimm. London: Hodder and Stoughton.

Problems

Introduction

Sometimes it seems we spend most of our teaching life searching for just the right problems, just the right books, just the right materials. Doing so is important, but we also need to know what engages the group, how they become involved with problems, and what kinds of questions they ask as they investigate shapes or data or numbers. It takes more than an interesting problem to construct a mathematical culture in the classroom.

One of the best ways to begin is to try out some low-risk, high-yield problems with your students to see what kinds of talk emerge and how they apply to your teaching and their learning.

If you work with younger students, there is a wealth of good questions and problems in the readings section of this book. The handshake problem in "Levels of Knowing 2: 'The Handshake'" (page 43) is a simple, classic problem that can be done with children as young as seven or eight. This is a wonderful place to begin, if you are willing to support lots of talk and many written and drawn representations. We also suggest you try the "Twos and Threes" investigation described in Section 2 (see page 27). When Ms. A asks her students to tell her all they can about those numbers, she is surprised at the variety of responses, and you may be too. This kind of activity is an excellent opportunity to listen to students and spend time hearing what they know. The problem focusing on caterpillars and butterflies (see Section 2, page 18) is also good for this.

In "Improving the Quality of Learning by Asking 'Good' Questions" (page 129), Peter Sullivan's simple, elegant rephrasings of ordinary mathematics questions are a great model; you may find them enough to get you moving toward richer discussion with your students. If you use those questions, they will likely become automatic after a while, and you may find they creep into many other subject areas, too.

Marion Walter's work ("Curriculum Topics Through Problem Posing," page 141) is full of good ideas. The investigations she starts with teachers and students are exciting and very open ended. Her other publications, some of which are included in the resource list, also contain excellent ideas for investigation and exploration.

It isn't necessary to overwhelm yourself searching for a perfect problem. There are many good questions and good investigations available; new curriculums such as TERC's *Used Numbers* (Dale Seymour 1990) and *Investigations in Data, Number, and Space* (Dale Seymour 1994) contain wonderful sustained investigations. Marilyn Burns has a wealth of replacement units that can be used in classrooms (see *Math by All Means* as an example); Educational Development Corporation has published a number of excellent units for the upper grades and middle schools. You certainly have favorites, as well—our resource list is quite selective and by no means exhaustive, so if we've left off your favorite, that doesn't mean we consider it "second best."

In this section are three problems for upper-grade students (third or fourth and up), that have produced interesting talk and sometimes quirky results, and that definitely engage students' interest and curiosity. We suggest you try one, two, or all three in your classroom (one at a time, of course). "Strange Happenings" extends students' experiences in looking for patterns and making generalizations about them. "Pyramids" is also focused on finding patterns and making generalizations; in addition, it brings up issues of terminology and vocabulary. "Billiard Ball Trajectories" appeals especially to fourth graders and above.

To deepen your own mathematical explorations, you might find a group of interested colleagues and do these problems together. They have rich potential for adult enjoyment—especially if you push yourselves to look deeply at each one. Wondering *why* a number pattern holds in "Strange Happenings" and under what conditions it might not, asking why there seem to be two ways of looking at the shapes in the "Pyramids" problem, exploring some of the patterns in "Billiard Ball Trajectories," will develop your understanding and your reasoning. In any case, whether you investigate them by yourself or with others, these problems are likely to provide some satisfying mathematical moments. We know you will enjoy them.

Strange Happenings: A Problem on the Hundred Board

Overview

Students multiply numbers at the corners of squares of different dimensions (e.g., 2 numbers × 2 numbers, 3 numbers × 3 numbers) on the hundred board or the 0–99 board. They subtract the products and look for patterns, making predictions about differences in larger squares.

Materials

Worksheet (Figure 7)
Calculators

Discussion

This problem focuses on finding patterns and making predictions and generalizations based on those patterns. Reasoning by extending patterns is an essential part of human thought. Humans notice patterns in their environments (people we recognize, recurrent events) in order to survive. In mathematics, finding, analyzing, and extending patterns is a central activity.

There are rich opportunities for talk as students work together on this problem. It's important that you have already done the problem so that you can explain it clearly and anticipate some of your students' questions. Be ready to reexplain and give examples of what students need to focus on. Usually students work most productively in pairs or threesomes; they can then come together for a whole-group discussion to compare their results and ask more questions.

This problem encourages students to look for patterns and use them to make predictions. Students discover a pattern in the intervals between differences (see Figure 8) and use the pattern to make predictions about 6-by-6 squares and 10-by-10 squares.

After your students have worked in small groups, have them compare their generalizations in a large-group summary discussion. A good summarizing question is, What written statements will allow you to predict the difference for any square? There are many ways of writing or drawing the same relationships, and students will enjoy seeing what others have done and checking to see whether they hold true.

STRANGE HAPPENINGS

```
  0    1    2    3    4    5    6 ·  7    8    9
 10  (11)  12  (13)  14   15   16   17   18   19
 20   21   22   23   24   25  (26)  27  (28)  29
 30  (31)  32  (33)  34   35   36   37   38   39
 40   41   42   43   44   45  (46)  47  (48)  49
 50   51   52   53   54   55   56   57   58   59
 60   61   62   63  (64)  65  (66)  67   68   69
 70  [71] [72]  73   74   75   76   77   78   79
 8C  [81] [82]  83  (84)  85  (86)  87   88   89
 90   91   92   93   94   95   96   97   98   99
```

1. For each 3 by 3 (those using circles)

   a. Multiply the two pairs of numbers connected by a line.
   b. Record in the table below.
   c. Subtract the smaller product from the larger product. Record.
   d. Repeat these steps with a 3 by 3 of your own.

	Product	Product	Difference
1			
2			
3			
Your own			

What did you discover?

_____

_____

_____

_____

2. Try different sizes. Record the difference between the products. A 2 by 2 is shown using squares.

Size	2 by 2	3 by 3	4 by 4	5 by 5
Difference				

3. Predict the result of a 6 by 6. _____ Check your prediction.

4. Predict the result of a 10 by 10. _____ Check your prediction.

FIG. 7 From Problem Solving in Mathematics Grade 5. *Copyrighted 1983 by Lane Education Service District. Available from Dale Seymour Publications, Palo Alto, CA 94303. Reprinted by permission.*

Size	2 by 2	3 by 3	4 by 4	5 by 5
Difference	10	40	90	160
Difference between differences		30	50	70

FIG. 8   Patterns in the differences.

Extensions

This is a problem that lends itself to what if? questions. You can extend your students' thinking by focusing on two of the problem constraints:

1. The problem is limited to squares. Would the results be patterned if you looked at rectangles? What are the patterns of the differences between *those* diagonals? Are there other quadrilaterals that yield interesting patterns? Encourage students to try a variety of other shapes.
2. The dimensions of the board are 10 by 10. Can you investigate a 12-by-12 square on a grid that's 10 squares wide? What would a 12-by-12 board look like? Rearrange the board. Do relationships change? How do the patterns on a 6-by-6 board (see Figure 9) differ from those on the 10-by-10 arrangement?

This problem also encourages investigations of our number system. Because the number system is straightforward and systematic, it produces many patterns and relationships. The patterns here link number and shape. Your students may want to test conjectures about other spatial and numerical relationships. For example:

1. Does this pattern hold true for squares drawn on the calendar?
2. What would happen if we arranged the numerals in a triangular format?

0	1	2	3	4	5
6	7	8	9	10	11
12	13	14	15	16	17
18	19	20	21	22	23
24	25	26	27	28	29
30	31	32	33	34	35

FIG. 9   A 6-by-6 grid.

Pyramids: Points and Corners

Overview

In this investigation of pyramids, students look for and identify relationships among the elements of triangular, square, pentagonal, and hexag-
onal pyramids. They describe the relationships in written statements
and determine whether they hold true for all pyramids.

Materials

Pyramids worksheet (Figure 10)
Models of pyramids, preferably constructed by students

Discussion

This investigation is best done in two parts. First, spend a class session
constructing pyramids. Although the worksheet includes perspective
drawings, even fifth and sixth graders profit from having the solid figures
available as they work on this problem. Building the figures allows
students to be thoroughly familiar with the shapes and helps them
analyze patterns more thoughtfully.

PYRAMIDS

Pyramids have a point, faces that are triangles and bottoms that can have different shapes. A pyramid gets its name from the shape of the bottom.

| Triangular | Square | Pentagonal | Hexagonal |

1. Use the drawings to help you fill in the table.

Pyramid Name	Number of sides in the bottom	Number of faces including the bottom	Number of corners	Number of edges
Triangular				6
Square		5		
Pentagonal	5			
Hexagonal			7	

2. Answer these by looking for patterns in the table.

   If the bottom of a pyramid has

   a. 8 sides, it has _____ faces.

   b. 13 sides, it has _____ corners.

   c. 50 sides, it has _____ edges.

3. Look for other patterns in the table. Write them on the back of this paper.

FIG. 10   *From* Problem Solving in Mathematics Grade 5. *Copyrighted 1983 by Lane Education Service District. Available from Dale Seymour Publications, Palo Alto, CA 94303. Reprinted by permission.*

In a second session, ask small groups of three or four to use their models as they work in the activities on Figure 10. After they have developed some general statements of relationships they see, conduct a whole-class discussion where groups present their generalizations to each other. Encourage the class to test each other's statements and see whether they all agree about their truth. This kind of testing and agreement is at the heart of a community's construction of mathematics.

Finding patterns and describing the many relationships that exist among the faces, edges, vertices, and other features of pyramids is the ostensible focus, but you may also want to highlight definitional disagreements. Thinking about different uses of similar terms helps students focus on convincing others—the beginning of mathematical proof. Our experience with this activity (with both adults and children) has been that definitional differences often emerge; the resolution of these differences is an excellent opportunity for mathematical talk.

Your group may well discover that they are using the terms *point* and *corner* differently. Is a point the same as a corner? Is a corner a point? Should we count corners as points and points as corners? It's important to let this discussion take place; mathematics is full of this kind of disagreement. People must think about how to resolve differences and test definitions. It's not something for you to resolve *for* your students. If you moderate the discussion but don't intervene except to suggest questions, this activity can produce interesting and intense attempts to convince—again, the beginning of mathematical proof.

Bumping into a disagreement is a good example of how mathematicians discover that they need to develop shared definitions of terms. Definitions are not always constructed in advance; it's only when they make a difference in results that they *must* be clarified.

Listen as a group of students argue with each other in a fifth-grade classroom:

Michael: We should change our definition to say an edge is a place where faces meet. I know it in my head, but I can't say it.
Nia: But it *is* a point so why can't they call it a point instead of edges, faces, or whatever?
Harold: Listen! Because they have a different meaning for point.
Deborah: Look at the dictionary.
Nia: I know, but this *is* a point. So why can't they call it a point?

Discussions like this one trigger issues of mathematical authority. Is the dictionary right? Is its definition reasonable? Should we look in a glossary? Students will learn that they can have different ideas about meanings, and they will wrestle with finding an appropriate term.

Giving them the term *vertex* would have relieved them of this wrangle. But we found that students who thought about how the meanings made a difference later realized that *vertex* was the term they needed. The dissonance stayed with them, they knew they needed a larger term that incorporated both of the others, and they recognized it when they found it. What could be a better mathematical lesson than that?

Billiard Ball Trajectories

"Billiard Ball Trajectories" (Figure 11) is one of our favorite problems. It has engaged many teachers and students in interesting and productive talk. In order to keep the discussion going, your students have to find ways to articulate and record relationships that they see clearly. They begin to realize that plain English sentences or pictures or formulas are all valid ways to do that.

Problems like this are key features of Harold Jacobs's *Mathematics: A Human Endeavor* (W. H. Freeman 1970). The book was originally written for high school students, but elementary teachers found that many of the problems in it appealed to younger students as well. Doing problems like these encourages students to offer conjectures and test hypotheses. They blend geometry and number.

Overview

Students create rectangular arrays of different dimensions and investigate how size affects the path of a billiard ball given certain constraints. The different-sized tables are sorted. A characterization of what happens with different-sized rectangles is the focus of the investigation. The emphasis here is on creating a collection of tables that share specific characteristics and on making generalizations about them.

Materials

Graph paper
Scissors and glue
Straightedges or rulers

A ball bounces off the sides of a billiard table. It always bounces off at the same angle it hits the wall, and it always starts in the lower left-hand corner at an angle of 45°. It doesn't stop until it starts to retrace its path. (Sometimes that means it will reverse itself; sometimes it will start over again.)

If the ball crosses every square on the table, the table is called "interesting"; if it does not cross each square, it is called "boring."

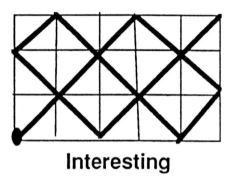

Interesting

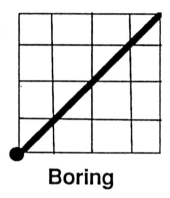

Boring

Draw different-sized billiard tables on graph paper.

With your group, make a collection of ten interesting billiard tables and a collection of ten boring ones.

- What patterns do you see?
- What conjectures or generalizations can you make?
- How might the size and shape of the rectangle relate to whether it's boring or interesting?

You may want to explore tables of different shapes (L-shaped tables or triangular ones).

FIG. 11   Billiard ball trajectories.

Discussion

As you can see in Figure 11, the billiard tables are sorted into two categories, interesting or boring, depending on whether the ball's path crosses every square on the table or only some of the squares. The ball starts in the lower left-hand corner at 45 degrees and goes in a straight line across squares until it reaches an edge. Then the ball bounces off the edge at 90 degrees to its previous path; the angle of incidence is equal to the angle of reflection. It keeps going until it begins to retrace its path. If the ball goes directly into a corner, it bounces back out along the same line.

Although we often say that mathematics should relate to real life, this problem may relate a little too much to real life for some students. It focuses on an *abstraction* of the behavior of a billiard ball; it isn't subject to the real laws of physics. If that makes it confusing for some students, it's a good opportunity to differentiate between mathematics that is literally connected to the real world and mathematics that is abstracted from real phenomena.

This investigation generates conjectures that students can test. At first, small groups of students make tables, trace the balls' paths, and sort tables into collections; after each small group has a collection of ten interesting and ten boring tables, they can begin to make generalizations about the characteristics of each. When they bring their generalizations to the large group for discussion, conjectures and predictions take over.

This problem brings up many wonderful areas of mathematics. You are likely to find it as engaging as the students do. What is the central idea of this problem? Ratio and proportion are involved in every aspect. Some teachers see it as being about greatest common factor; others see it as reducing fractions; still others see it as an exercise in division (analyzing remainders is surely modular arithmetic). Teachers who look at the problem with a visual bent often see it as one of scale; those who love patterns see it as reducing a design to its basic form.

Pattern-finders are likely to become involved in thinking about what some students call "the four basic design types." Will those ever change? How does changing the shape of the table change the results?

Resource List

Mathematical Talk

Children's talk, like all communication, needs an audience, an intent, and a speaker. These references will help you think about creating a community of discourse in your classroom.

Barnes, D. 1992. *From Conversation to Curriculum*. 2d ed. Portsmouth, NH: Boynton/Cook.

Cobb, P. 1992. "Interaction and Learning in Mathematics Classroom Situations." *Educational Studies in Mathematics* 23 (1): 99–122.

Corwin, R. B. 1993. "Doing Mathematics Together: Creating a Mathematical Culture." *Arithmetic Teacher* 40 (6) (February): 338–42.

Countryman, J. 1992. *Writing to Learn Mathematics: Strategies That Work, K–12*. Portsmouth, NH: Heinemann.

Duckworth, E. 1987. *The Having of Wonderful Ideas*. New York: Teachers College Press.

Gallas, K. 1994. *The Languages of Learning: How Children Talk, Write, Dance, Draw, and Sing Their Understanding of the World*. New York: Teachers College Press.

Ginsburg, H. 1982. *Children's Arithmetic: How They Learn It and How You Teach It*. Austin, TX: Pro–Ed.

Griffiths, R. & M. Clyne. 1994. *Language in the Mathematics Classroom: Talking, Representing, Recording*. Portsmouth, NH: Heinemann.

Jensen, R. J. (ed.) 1993. *Research Ideas for the Classroom: Early Childhood Mathematics*. New York: Macmillan.

Paley, V. G. 1981. *Wally's Stories*. Cambridge, MA: Harvard University Press.

———. 1986. "On Listening to What the Children Say." *Harvard Educational Review* 56 (2) (May): 122–131.

Pierce, K. M. & C. J. Gilles (eds.) 1993. *Cycles of Meaning: Exploring the Potential of Talk in Learning Communities*. Portsmouth, NH: Heinemann.

Pimm, D. (ed.) 1988. *Mathematics, Teachers and Children*. London: Hodder and Stoughton.

Russell, S. J. & R. B. Corwin. 1993. "Talking Mathematics: 'Going Slow' and 'Letting Go.'" *Phi Delta Kappan* 74 (7) (March): 555–58.

RESOURCE LIST

.... 161

Sullivan, P. & D. Clarke. 1991. *Communication in the Classroom: The Importance of Good Questioning*. Geelong, Victoria, Australia: Deakin University Press.

Teaching and Learning

There are many different approaches to looking at and learning about children's mathematical thinking and ways of supporting it. These represent only a small part of the work that is available to mathematics educators.

Cobb, P. 1991. "Reconstructing Elementary School Mathematics." *Focus on Learning Problems in Mathematics* 13 (2): 3–32.

Cooney, T. J. & C. R. Hirsch (eds.) 1990. *Teaching and Learning Mathematics in the 1990s* (1990 Yearbook). Reston, VA: National Council of Teachers of Mathematics.

Dewey, J. 1990. *The School and Society and The Child and the Curriculum: A Centennial Edition*. Chicago: The University of Chicago Press.

Duckworth, E. 1987. *The Having of Wonderful Ideas*. New York: Teachers College Press.

Ginsburg, H. P. 1983. *The Development of Mathematical Thinking*. New York: Academic Press.

Good, T., D. A. Grouws, & H. Ebmeier. 1983. *Active Mathematics Teaching.* New York: Longman.

Greene, M. 1991. "Teaching: The Question of Personal Reality." In *Staff Development for Education in the 90's: New Demands, New Realities, New Perspectives*, ed. L. Lieberman & L. Miller. New York: Teachers College Press.

Hawkins, D. 1980. "Nature, Man, and Mathematics." In *The Informed Vision*, D. Hawkins. NY: Pantheon Press.

Hiebert, J. 1984. "Children's Mathematics Learning: The Struggle to Link Form and Understanding." *Elementary School Journal* 84 (May): 496–513.

———— (ed.) 1986. *Conceptual and Procedural Knowledge: The Case of Mathematics*. Hillsdale, NJ: Lawrence Erlbaum Associates.

Land, F. W. 1963. *The Language of Mathematics*. Garden City, NY: Doubleday.

Papert, S. 1980. *Mindstorms: Children, Computers, and Powerful Ideas*. New York: Basic Books.

Piaget, J. 1972. *To Understand Is to Invent*. New York: Grossman.

Rowe, M. B. 1986. "Wait Time: Slowing Down May Be a Way of Speeding Up!" *Journal of Teacher Education* (January-February): 43–50.

Schön, D. A. 1983. *The Reflective Practitioner: How Professionals Think in Action*. New York: Basic Books.

Steen, L. 1990. *On the Shoulders of Giants*. Washington, DC: National Academy Press.

Swetz, F. J. (ed.) 1994. *From Five Fingers to Infinity: A Journey Through the History of Mathematics*. Chicago: Open Court.

Stigler, J. W. 1990. *Mathematical Knowledge of Japanese, Chinese, and American Elementary School Children*. Reston, VA: National Council of Teachers of Mathematics.

Vygotsky, L. 1978. *Mind in Society*, ed. by M. Cole, V. John-Steiner, S. Scribner, and E. Souberman. Cambridge, MA: Harvard University Press.

Vygotsky, L. 1978. *Mind in Society*, ed. by M. Cole, V. John-Steiner, S. Scribner, and E. Souberman. Cambridge, MA: Harvard University Press.

Whitehead, A. N. 1929. *The Aims of Education and Other Essays*. New York: Macmillan.

Wheatley, G H. 1991. "Constructivist Perspectives on Science and Mathematics Learning." *Science Education* 75: 9–21.

Teaching and Curriculum

There are many wonderful references in mathematics teaching. Here we include the classics, the ones we know will provide solid, interesting starting points for building your curriculum.

Atkinson, S. (ed.) 1992. *Mathematics with Reason*. Portsmouth, NH: Heinemann.

Baratta-Lorton, M. 1976. *Mathematics Their Way*. Palo Alto, CA: Addison-Wesley.

Barnett, C. S., D. Goldenstein & B. Jackson. 1994. *Mathematics Teaching Cases: Fractions, Decimals, Ratios, and Percents*. Portsmouth, NH: Heinemann.

Brannan, R. & O. Schaaf, Directors. 1983. *The Lane County Mathematics Project: Problem Solving in Mathematics, Grade 5*. Palo Alto: Dale Seymour Publications.

Brown, S. & M. Walter. 1983. *The Art of Problem Posing*. Hillsdale, NJ: Lawrence Erlbaum Associates, Inc.

Burns, M. 1992. *About Teaching Mathematics: A K–8 Resource*. Sausalito, CA: Marilyn Burns Education Associates.

Burns, M. 1991. *Math By All Means*. Sausalito, CA: Marilyn Burns Education Associates.

Corwin, R. B., S. J. Russell & C. C. Tierney. 1991. *Seeing Fractions: A Unit for the Upper Elementary Grades*. Sacramento, CA: California Department of Education.

Corwin, R. B. & S. N. Friel. 1990. *Used Numbers—Statistics: Prediction and Sampling*. Palo Alto, CA: Dale Seymour Publications.

Cundy, H. M. & A. P. Rollett. 1961. *Mathematical Models*. 2nd ed. Oxford, UK: Clarendon Press.

Friel, S. N., J. R. Mokros & S. J. Russell. 1992. *Used Numbers—Statistics: Middles, Means, and In-Betweens*. Palo Alto, CA: Dale Seymour Publications.

Holden, A. 1971. *Shapes, Space, and Symmetry*. New York: Columbia University Press.

Jacobs, H. R. 1970. *Mathematics: a Human Endeavor. A Textbook for Those Who Think They Don't Like the Subject*. San Francisco: W. H. Freeman.

Labinowicz, E. 1988. *Learning from Children: New Beginnings for Teaching Numerical Thinking*. Menlo Park, CA: Addison-Wesley.

Parker, R. E. 1994. *Mathematical Power: Lessons From a Classroom*. Portsmouth, NH: Heinemann.

Reid, C. 1994. *From Zero to Infinity: What Makes Numbers Interesting*. 3d ed. New York: Crowell.

Richardson, K. 1990. *A Look at Childrens' Thinking: Assessment Videos for K–2 Mathematics*. Norman, OK: Educational Enrichment.

Rowan, T. & B. Bourne. 1994. *Thinking Like Mathematicians: Putting the K–4 NCTM Standards into Practice*. Portsmouth, NH: Heinemann.

Russell, S. J. & R. B. Corwin. 1990. *Used Numbers—Sorting: Groups and Graphs*. Palo Alto, CA: Dale Seymour Publications.

————. 1991. *Used Numbers—Statistics: The Shape of the Data*. Palo Alto, CA: Dale Seymour Publications.

Schools Council. 1976. *Early Experiences*. New York: Macdonald Educational.

————. 1976. *Science from Toys: Stages 1 and 2*. New York: Macdonald Educational.

————. 1976. *Ourselves*. New York: Macdonald Educational.

TERC. 1994. *Investigations in Data, Number, and Space*. Palo Alto, CA: Dale Seymour Publications. [Titles include *Mathematical Thinking at Grade 4*, *Exploring Solids and Boxes*, *Landmarks in the Hundreds*, *Things that Come in Groups*.]

Tsuruda, G. 1993. *Putting it Together: Middle School Math in Transition*. Portsmouth, NH: Heinemann.

Williams, E. & H. Shuard. 1970. *Elementary Mathematics Today: A Resource for Teachers, Grades 1–8*. Menlo Park, CA: Addison-Wesley. (Out of print, but worth finding.)

Wenninger, M. J. 1971. *Polyhedron Models*. Cambridge, UK: Cambridge University Press.

NCTM Standards

This is the right time for a membership in the National Council of Teachers of Mathematics, a central source of information about developments in the mathematics community. Their publications are extremely helpful.

Curcio, F. R. (ed.) 1991. *Curriculum and Evaluation Standards for School Mathematics: Addenda Series, Grades 5–8*. Reston, VA: National Council of Teachers of Mathematics.

Leiva, M. A. (ed.) 1991–93. *Curriculum and Evaluation Standards for School Mathematics: Addenda Series, Grades K–6*. Reston, VA: National Council of Teachers of Mathematics.

National Council of Teachers of Mathematics. 1989. *Curriculum and Evaluation Standards for School Mathematics*. Reston, VA: National Council of Teachers of Mathematics.

————. 1991. *Professional Standards for Teaching Mathematics*. Reston, VA: National Council of Teachers of Mathematics.

Suppliers

The catalogs of these publishers and distributors are a powerful means of keeping up with the field of elementary mathematics. In them you will find many resources to help you do mathematics, teach mathematics, and reflect on your students' learning.

You may want to pool your catalog collections with your colleagues and set up a resource center in your faculty room.

Activity Resources Company, Inc.
P. O. Box 4875
Hayward, CA 94540
(510) 782-1300
FAX: (510) 787-8172

Creative Publications
5040 West 111th Street
Oak Lawn, IL 60453
(800) 624-0822

Cuisenaire Company of America, Inc.
P.O. Box 5026
White Plains, NY 10601-5026
Customer Service: (800) 237-3142
FAX: (800) 551-RODS
Internet: INFO@CUISENAIRE.COM

Dale Seymour Publications
P.O. Box 10888
Palo Alto, CA 94303-0879
(800) 872-1100
FAX: (415) 324-3424

Delta Education, Inc.
P.O. Box 3000
Nashua, NH 03061-3000
(800) 442-5444
FAX (800) 282-9560

Didax, Inc.
Education Resources
395 Main Street
Rowley, MA 01969
(800) 458-0024

ETA (Educational Teaching Aids)
620 Lakeview Parkway
Vernon Hills, IL 60061
(800) 445-5985

GEMS, Lawrence Hall of Science
University of California
Berkeley, CA 94720
(510) 642-7771

Heinemann
361 Hanover Street
Portsmouth, NH 03801-3912
(800) 541-2086
FAX: (800) 847-0938

Key Curriculum Press
2512 Martin Luther King Jr. Way
P.O. Box 2304
Berkeley, CA 94702
(800) 338-7638

Minnesota Educational Computing Company (MECC)
Brookdale Corporate Center
6160 Summit Drive
Minneapolis, MN 55430-4003
(800) 685-6322

National Council of Teachers of Mathematics
1906 Association Drive
Reston, VA 22091
(800) 235-7566

Scott Resources
P.O. Box 2121
Ft. Collins, CO 80522
(800) 289-9299

Watten/Poe Teaching Resource Center
P.O. Box 1509
San Leandro, CA 94577
(800) 833-3389
FAX: (800) 972-7722

Credits

"Levels of Knowing 2: 'The Handshake' " by Jeannie Billington and Pat Evans was originally published in *Mathematics Teaching* 120 (September 1987). Reprinted by permission of the authors.

"Writing to Learn" reprinted by permission of Joan Countryman: WRITING TO LEARN MATHEMATICS: STRATEGIES THAT WORK, K–12 (Heinemann, A division of Reed Elsevier Inc., Portsmouth, NH, 1992).

"Learning in Breadth and Depth" reprinted by permission of the publisher from Duckworth, Eleanor, THE HAVING OF WONDERFUL IDEAS. (New York: Teachers College Press, © 1987 by Teachers College, Columbia University. All rights reserved.).

"I, Thou, and It" originally appeared in THE INFORMED VISION by David Hawkins. Copyright © 1980. Published by Pantheon. Reprinted by permission of the author.

"Tensions" by John Mason was originally published in *Mathematics Teaching* 114 (March 1986). Reprinted by permission of the author.

"On Listening to What the Children Say" by Vivian Gussin Paley, was originally published in *Harvard Educational Review*, 56:2, pp. 122–131. Copyright © 1986 by the President and Fellows of Harvard College. All rights reserved.

"Improving the Quality of Learning by Asking 'Good' Questions" by Peter Sullivan from COMMUNICATION IN THE CLASSROOM: THE IMPORTANCE OF GOOD QUESTIONING by Peter Sullivan and David

Math Excursions Series
Project-Based Mathematics

Donna Burk, George Miner School
Allyn Snider, Wilsonville Primary School
Paula Symonds, San Francisco Day School

The *Math Excursions Series* is a set of clearly organized, thoroughly field-tested units for primary teachers who want an innovative extension of mathematics beyond the pages of a workbook into art, literature, science, and social studies. Each unit is an exciting departure from the main road of systematic math instruction, an opportunity to drop daily math routines and venture into real-world problem solving for a week or more. There are three books in the series, each specific to the grade it features.

Math Excursions K

In this unit, kindergartners sort through many buttons in a class button hunt. They experiment with a variety of two- and three-dimensional shapes to see which works best for a house. Paths are created and tested, eggs counted, beds made for sick teddy bears, and much more. Math concepts range from geometry, measurement, and sorting to sequencing, patterning, and counting.

0-435-08345-7 / 266pp / Spiral-bound

Math Excursions 1

First graders create their own hats, explore counting patterns through a series of traditional folk tales and nursery rhymes, figure out how to collect and share a large amount of candy, write their own story problems, and create story maps to retell *The Three Billy Goats Gruff.* Math concepts range from geometry, measurement, and sorting to estimation, patterning, and computation.

0-435-08331-7 / 259pp / Spiral-bound

Math Excursions 2

Second graders explore and create patchwork quiltblocks of growing complexity, investigate the common properties of quart containers, plan a party for a hundred people, write their own story problems, and build a model village. Math concepts range from geometry, measurement, and sorting to estimation, patterning, and computation.

0-435-08321-X / 218pp / Spiral-bound

For more information about these books, call 1-800-541-2086, fax 1-800-847-0938, or write: Heinemann, 361 Hanover Street, Portsmouth, NH 03801-3912.

Mathematical Power
Lessons from a Classroom
Ruth E. Parker, Collaborative Learning Associates
Foreword by Kathy Richardson

"Veteran teachers will see on these pages enlightening images of their own struggles. For novices this book is an enticing invitation to participate in mathematics reform."
— Teaching Children Mathematics

Mathematical Power is a book that shows how to bring the goals of the NCTM *Standards* to life in a classroom on a day-to-day basis. Although it is the story of one classroom, the implications go far beyond this classroom.

As the teachers here struggle to examine their practices, teachers will connect with them and gain a clearer picture of what it means to teach mathematics for understanding. These teachers turn theory into actual classroom practice while addressing the complexities of selecting new mathematics content; planning for instruction; establishing a collaborative learning environment; helping children learn to make choices and take responsibility for their learning; meeting the academic and social needs of all children; keeping records of children's work; and assessing for understanding.

Ruth Parker brings to this book an in-depth understanding of the goals of mathematics reform efforts, a belief in children as caring and powerful sense makers, and a long history of working to make schools more relevant and meaningful places for children and teachers.

0-435-08339-2 / 229pp / Paper

Thinking like Mathematicians
Putting the K-4 NCTM *Standards* into Practice
Thomas Rowan, University of Maryland, College Park
Barbara Bourne, University of Maryland, Baltimore County

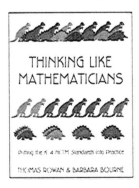

"This new book is on the top of my list."
— Teaching Children Mathematics

Teachers already implementing the NCTM *Standards* are discovering that their students are not intimidated by math, but are confident, creative, and actively involved in the process.

Strategies used in these classrooms are modeled throughout *Thinking like Mathematicians*. Through vignettes and anecdotes, readers meet children who are problem solvers; who are confident of their ability to meet the challenges of complex and meaningful mathematical tasks; who can reason mathematically; who value the role of mathematics in their daily lives; and who are learning to communicate their understandings to their peers and teachers. Readers also meet the teachers who have planned for and are implementing the programs that facilitate these mathematics learning processes.

The authors combine their training and experience in mathematics, early childhood education, and child-centered curriculum development to present a showcase for the real experts— the teachers and children of classrooms where students are constructing their own mathematics knowledge, gaining "math power," and ultimately thinking like mathematicians.

0-435-08343-0 / 134pp / Paper

Mathematics in Process
Ann and Johnny Baker

"The strength of this book is the connection that it makes between process writing and process mathematics . . ."
—The Reading Teacher

Mathematics in Process is written to develop and extend a confidence in mathematics that teachers already feel in language arts. The purposes and conditions of natural learning, now common in the language classroom, are applied to learning and doing mathematics. The emphasis is on encouraging elementary children to try for themselves, letting them develop and compare math strategies in situations that are meaningful and important. This involves enabling children to develop their own approaches, work collaboratively on mathematics, communicate their findings, and reflect on what they have learned.

This book encourages teachers to share in children's excitement when mathematics is in process and shows that the approach provides a means of unlocking mathematics creatively in every child.

0-435-08306-6 / 170pp / Paper

Maths in the Mind
A Process Approach to Mental Strategies
Ann and Johnny Baker

"The Bakers show us that children, using what they do know to approach the answer in a perhaps unconventional but nonetheless correct way, develop confidence in their ability as problem solvers."
—Connect

Maths in the Mind suggests starting points for encouraging elementary children to become fluent and independent thinkers in the math lesson. The authors present ideas for building on strategies that children acquire naturally before they come to school, and outline additional strategies that children develop as they become more competent at mathematics.

The book's two sections provide guidelines to help teachers implement a "maths in the mind" approach. Part One gives the background and provides a description of math strategies that researchers have observed both children and adults use. Part Two then describes twenty activities that encourage maths in the mind, suggesting ways they might be used and extended in the classroom. These activities promote a relaxed environment where "risk taking" rather than the "right answer" is appreciated and supported.

0-435-08316-3 / 120pp / Paper

For more information about these books, call 1-800-541-2086, fax 1-800-847-0938, or write: Heinemann, 361 Hanover Street, Portsmouth, NH 03801-3912.